STAKEHOLDER POWER

STAKEHOLDER POWER

POWER

A Winning Strategy for Building
Stakeholder Commitment and
Driving Corporate Growth

STEVEN F. WALKER

JEFFREY W. MARR

PERSEUS PUBLISHING
Cambridge, Massachusetts

Many of the designations used by manufacturers and sellers to distinguish their products are claimed as trademarks. Where those designations appear in this book and Perseus Publishing was aware of a trademark claim, the designations have been printed in initial capital letters.

A CIP record for this book is available from the Library of Congress.
Copyright © 2001 by Steven F. Walker
ISBN:0-7382-0389-0

Perseus Publishing is a member of the Perseus Books Group
Find Perseus Publishing on the World Wide Web at
http://www.perseuspublishing.com

Perseus Publishing books are available at special discounts for bulk purchases in the U.S. by corporations, institutions, and other organizations. For more information, please contact the Special Markets Department at the Perseus Books Group, 11 Cambridge Center, Cambridge, MA, or call 617-252-5298.

Text design by Heather Hutchison
Set in 11-point Garamond Book by Perseus Publishing Services

1 2 3 4 5 6 7 8 9 10—03 02 01
First printing, May 2001

To Dorothy "Tommie" Walker Anderson and Frank D. Walker—the only role models I ever needed, in business and in life.   —SW

To Robert M. Marr, my first great teacher of important values, and John W. Welsh, who proved again that you can build a great company without losing sight of your principles.   —JM

Contents

Preface

It has been more than five years since the first person suggested to us that we "write a book." Perhaps that person was tired of listening to us talk about our experiences and this was a courteous way to end the conversation. Whatever it was, we took that suggestion and filed it away in the memory database. In the ensuing years, similar suggestions were made by others, and this caused us to think that maybe, just maybe, these people actually thought that there was some value in our ideas and the stories we told.

This book tells the secrets of stakeholder power. It is a story that shows that the best businesses are those run with both the heart and mind. Running a business with the heart implies that businesses do what is right and manage, not just the bottom line, but also the best interests of all those who interact with or have a stake in the business. We refer to these people as "stakeholders." But don't automatically categorize this book in the genre of "do-gooders." The bottom line of this story is that companies that adopt a stakeholder approach don't just make the world better by treating their stakeholders well, they are also rewarded with long-term, sustainable financial success.

In our combined business experience of nearly five decades, we have been able to work with some of the world's greatest companies.

From that, we have been struck by an ongoing paradox of the business world. How is it that one of the pillars of American society, corporations, which have played such an important role in our nation's history and created so much value for so many people, continue to suffer from such a poor reputation? Even now, after all the economic success our country has enjoyed, the popular media and culture continue to profess that "business" is bad and is inherently in conflict with the goals of individuals, communities, and society. All the while, our work continued to bring us to the opposite conclusion.

Most of the great business leaders we have met are highly principled people, and most successful businesses have an enormously helpful impact on society. At the same time, we know that some business approaches are unique in keeping people front and center to what they are really about. Corporations are differentiated by the way in which they treat their "stakeholders," and the way they treat stakeholders has a lot to do with how these stakeholders treat the company in return. Good companies get good treatment. We further discovered that the way in which companies and their stakeholders interact ("stakeholder relationships") has an impact on how these businesses perform financially. Companies with better stakeholder relationships perform better than those that don't have good relationships. Finally, we found lessons and best practices that can be drawn from various companies that can help other companies simultaneously improve their business performance, their business practices, and the quality of some important people's lives.

These profound discoveries, reiterated time after time, company after company, engagement after engagement, caused us to begin to articulate the ideas that would become this book. It is a story we knew could help business people rediscover some basic truths in a fast-moving and very complex business world. It is a story about clear issues and harmony, instead of ambiguity and confrontation. Yet, it really is a story about power, a power that every company can choose to harness if it wants to. There is a growing power in the hands of customers, associates, investors, and others influential in business to pick the firms they want to associate with. The process of understanding these basic relationships on which a business is built won't make every decision simpler. In fact, some will be more difficult, but the effort is worth it: Loyal, committed stakeholders sustain organizations.

We have seen only good things happen when companies focus in on, commit to, and truly believe in the power of building outstanding stakeholder relationships, as long as they maintain their core business and product values at the same time.

Stakeholder Power formally started in late 1999. Since neither one of us had ever written a book, we needed to understand the process. Steve took the first steps, learning how one goes about actually writing a book. He assembled the initial team that pulled together the proposal and connected with people who were knowledgeable in the field of business publishing.

This project remained at the concept and outline stage until Jeff entered the picture. It was Jeff who spent the time necessary to lead the content research, sift through all the information, organize it, rough out the chapter drafts, and fill in the gaps to create something meaningful.

As we got into the process, we found that a great deal of the concepts and raw material for the book already existed. For example, we had long been in the habit of writing up client case histories and white papers when we happened upon companies engaged in activities that supported our arguments. These proved to be very useful either for content or as examples of company profiles. We also had conducted several proprietary research studies, primarily to satisfy our intellectual curiosity but also with an eye toward furthering our belief that "stakeholder power" really existed. Then there was the treasure chest of clients that we have been blessed with and all the projects we have conducted over the last 20 or so years. And finally, all of the stories, anecdotes, and real people who have made this concept of stakeholder power come alive.

We hope you enjoy reading the book and that you learn many new ideas or ways of thinking about your business. If in some way it guides you to change something in your organization or gives you the courage to go ahead and do something you were already considering, we will know it was worth our effort. If you start to implement stakeholder power principles, we are convinced your business will enjoy more long-term sustainable success. And yes, the world will also be a little bit better place.

Stakeholder Power has its own group of stakeholders, and we would like to thank those without whom this book could not have been published. First of all, we'd like to thank our editor, Nick Philipson of Perseus Books, for his enthusiastic and never-ending challenges to make this book better. He stayed on us to meet deadlines and did not compromise when it came to the overall quality of the product. The key member of the early team was Bill Birchard, an accomplished author in his own right, with whom we had collaborated before and hope to again. Bill helped us write the proposal and also introduced us to Helen Rees, our literary agent. Helen was the early believer in the project who introduced us to Nick and Perseus. Marnie Maxwell, a local freelance editor, was our initial line of external review, and her input into the manuscript of novice writers was invaluable prior to sending it to Perseus. We also want to thank Bill Redgate and Tina Sullivan for taking the time to review and react to our initial drafts of the manuscript.

Turning our focus internally to Walker Information, there are literally hundreds of colleagues, both past and present, who influenced and contributed to pieces and parts of this book. First of all, we want to thank the Board of Directors of the company for believing in the project so strongly and allowing us some time away from our day jobs to complete it. Next, we need to single out Sandy Heil, who typed and retyped all 63,000 or so words and formatted and reformatted all of the exhibits and subtitles and other things that we learned "had to be done just so."

Now, by name, we'd like to thank some people who had a special role in creating content for the book or who had a hand in directly supporting the effort. These people include, but are not limited to, Ginny Angelovic, Doug Grisaffe, BJ Kyzr-Sheeley, Marc Drizin, Frank Walker, Jim Sammer, Pat Gibbons, Jill Russell, Laura Bayes, Vonda Gilley, and Bill Kaszubski.

We would also like to thank the customers of Walker Information who willingly offered their case histories to make this book a living example of how to use stakeholder power, as well as the other great companies that we learned about through other sources. Our thanks also go out to the members of the Walker Information Global Network around the world who contributed to the work on key accounts and the global proprietary studies that were used in this book.

Last, but certainly not least, we would each like to thank our individual families for their love and support. You know you are lucky when what you do for a living doesn't usually feel like work and when the joy your family brings reminds you to balance your life. We are both truly blessed with families who allow us to work hard in pursuit of our dreams and believe as we do that those dreams have a purpose well worth the effort.

The Power of Stakeholders

A Winning Plan for Building Stakeholder Commitment and Driving Corporate Growth

Transfer of Power and Overview

Although it might seem ironic, the highest-flying technology business of the "new economy" attributes its phenomenal success not just to technological innovation but to the way in which it deals with people, or with what we call "stakeholder power." That's right. Cisco Systems grew to become the world's most valuable enterprise in less than 16 years by offering computer networking solutions, to be sure, but also by mastering its individual and collective relationships with employees, customers, acquired executives, and other stakeholders. Simply put, Cisco has become a compelling place with which to do business.

1

Don't get us wrong: A ton of great ideas, strategy, leadership courage, and management acumen led to the phenomenal success of Cisco. But at the core of all that resides an incredible passion for the mission of the company, a mission subscribed to by each successive leader in its short history and by virtually all its employees and alliance partners. Cisco's mission is to help other companies network their computers for business solutions. They fulfill this mission by listening to and acting on customer desires, dreams, and requests. They acquire and hire smart people, grant them stock options and empower their teams with independence, equip them on the job, and focus everyone on customer impact. The Cisco teams work out solutions for customers that create incredible loyalty. The company also makes generous offers to business owners who sell to Cisco. Together their customers and acquirees reward the company with an even larger share of their already fast-growing expenditures in the networking solutions category. Their shareholders (including employees) have experienced an incredible run in the financial markets.

In addition to the commitment of employees, customers, and shareholders, Cisco has a reputation for tremendous loyalty to its suppliers, vendors, and business alliance partners. In return for that loyalty, the company demands (and gets) the same focus on the customer that it rewards in its employees. The company has become the acknowledged master of the merger/acquisition game, having completed more than 60 transactions since 1993 and retained executives from the merged companies at a rate well above average.

What Cisco has figured out, perhaps as well as any company in this new economy, is that fundamental shifts have occurred in the business landscape, which is now all about people and their commitment. The shifts in leverage brought about by the information revolution were predicted decades before Cisco was even founded, but it was Cisco that really mastered the business implications. This too can be called "stakeholder power": understanding the leverage of stakeholders better than your competitors do.

Stakeholder power isn't just for the high-tech, fast-growth companies because, as we demonstrate in this chapter, we're all in the new economy now. Organizations must learn and deploy the lessons learned by companies like Cisco. Although the centralized, hierarchical, command-and-control model seems to be yielding to what is in some ways a more complex organism of different stakeholders, business leaders will take some time learning to harness stakeholder power and build their companies around it.

It is time to believe in the change and adapt to it. We have entered an age in which competitors spring up from conceivably anywhere, where the points of selling and servicing are increasingly moving to the common ground arena of the World Wide Web. It is a world in which companies must understand customers' needs, because competitors offer their buyers more and more choices every day. And with social economists forecasting continued workforce shortages, businesses must not only accommodate the needs of employees but attract people of the right skills, develop them with training, or secure them through acquisition.

The era of stakeholder power has arrived, and it should become a core business strategy, complementing the product innovation, system upgrades, and financial objectives we build into our current and future plans.

The Stakeholder Imperative

Although it is not that difficult to envision a stakeholder focus in running a business, it is exceedingly difficult to implement such a focus. Corporate principles such as "safety first," "customer satisfaction," and "treat employees fairly" are often touted on plaques and in annual reports, but this book goes straight to the heart of meaningful relationships, which means earning people's commitment. Earning commitment in relationships is neither easy nor simple to sustain in business or our personal lives. But the outcome is well worth the journey. Corporate performance is what ultimately pleases the business owners or shareholders, but performance can be achieved in a fashion pleasing to our stakeholders as well. And the reverse is definitely true: When we have gained commitment from our stakeholders, it enhances our business performance, growth, and higher stock value over time.

The urgency of understanding stakeholders is motivated by the arrival of the "new economy," spawned from developing our fresh infrastructure of technology. Peter Drucker, who likes to call himself a "social ecologist," coined the term *knowledge worker* in 1959, predicting an evolution away from the industrial workplace as we knew it.[1] The traditional secrets to success—marshaling natural resources and the momentum of dominant market share—are no longer applicable. As Lester C. Thurow, a member of MIT's faculty and a business advisor, says, "Suddenly the answer is 'knowledge.' The knowledge-based economy is asking new questions, giving new answers, and developing new rules for success."[2] We have seen the resulting "new" part of the economy in the economic growth that has been spurred by this technical progress.

The chief economist at the Organization for Economic Cooperation and Development (OECD), Ignatio Visco, describes the "spill-over effects" of new technology, where the Internet and e-commerce enable the start-up of untold new enterprises as well as sizable efficiencies and other cost reduction opportunities for existing sectors.[3] Businesses of all types will benefit from what the spill-over technology sector has wrought, but they must make adjustments in their business cultures to win their quotient of available skilled workers and train others as needed.

Eaton Corp. is an $8.4 billion Cleveland-based industrial manufacturer, described in a June 2000 *Wall Street Journal* article as "a lion of the old economy." Eaton Chairman Stephen R. Hardis claims that the new and old economies aren't really all that different. After all, the new era companies are getting their comeuppance: Dot-coms are recognizing that profits really do matter, and Microsoft is facing the reality of an antitrust judgment. More significantly, the old-line companies are now adopting advanced technology to run their businesses more effectively. In the process, the old economy is not only showing signs of renewed growth but is suddenly competing with the new economy for knowledge workers.[4] All types of companies must change their ways to win loyalty from knowledge workers, and one day it appears we will all be knowledge workers!

If we are to understand the value of, and build relationships with, customers, employees, and other stakeholders, then we must adapt our business accounting. We must identify those constituents most valuable to the business. Chapter 2 explains the road to balancing shareholder and stakeholder value (the downsizing of the 1980s and 1990s and fixation with shareholder value being evidence of many businesses being out of balance).

We must reform our accounting systems so the intangible assets can be assessed accurately. We also must learn to measure such factors as relationship building, retention of various stakeholders, and metrics indicating the depth of commitment and the intentions of people to be loyal.

Not Just Relationship, But Commitment

Chapter 3 makes the case that business leaders—investors, business owners, boards of directors, and executives—should discover the right core values for the company, then ensure that those values are held by the organization as a whole. Any such values will include earning profits and building value for shareholders, but they must also address the needs of important constituencies of the business or stakeholder value.

The theme of building commitment and loyalty among constituents is further developed by explaining the underlying elements of successful business relationships. Relationships evolve through four different stages, beginning with others' awareness that your firm exists and ending with a desired action on their part. The ultimate goal of a business leader is to earn people's support. The nature of that support depends on the role of the individual as an interested citizen of the community, customer of the firm, supplier or other alliance partner, employee, investor, and so forth. No matter the type of stakeholder, the need to understand the depth of relationship and support from that stakeholder is important.

The nature of that support might also be called loyalty. But the goal of attaining true loyalty is a two-edged sword. True loyalty means not only gaining support from people's "feet" (whether they support us) but from their hearts and minds as well (what they think of us).

In Whom Do You Trust?

In the process of earning people's support in business relationships, one principle is the same as in personal relationships: We must first establish trust.

Chapter 4 explains how businesses are rediscovering the importance of integrity as an underpinning to business relationships. Visible integrity in the organization breeds trust and enables a strong corporate reputation to build over time. Maintaining integrity in business practices is unfortunately not as simple as setting a good example or assuming employees will behave in a certain way. It requires living out and teaching certain values, as well as using tools to measure progress and assess weaknesses in the integrity of the workplace.

One of the interesting new business trends to watch is the growth of ethics, compliance, or integrity management, as it becomes an important business function and profession.

The Customer Revolution

The revolution in stakeholder recognition has already begun. Arguably the first people touted as important business assets were customers. Just consider how *customer loyalty* has become an almost universal business mantra, as well as a performance metric. Customer loyalty is now the new millennium version of customer satisfaction as a corporate strategy. This idea symbolizes the significant trend noted by Michael Hammer, who refers to "the epochal shift in the world economy, as power has moved from sellers to buyers."[5]

The balance of power is shifting from seller to buyer because new technology and channels for purchasing have changed the expectations of customers. Companies now have the ability to register buying patterns and preferences of individual customers into databases that provide better service. In Chapter 5, the explosive growth of customer relationship management (CRM) systems is discussed along with the importance of individual (one-to-one) marketing and assessing customer loyalty.

Customer leverage also has the hidden power of converting entire business channels. Customer-driven technology has forced the changing of entire buying channels in retailing and business-to-business, sometimes ushering in a new set of suppliers because existing ones have difficulty changing. The winners are those more willing to convert their businesses, even to the point of "cannibalizing" themselves. Charles Schwab and Company, the firm that popularized discount brokerage services and later shifted its business to online transactions with even deeper discounts, epitomizes "knowing one's customers." Schwab knew the evolving needs of investors well enough to reinvent the business around them, to the point where the new business took away from the old sources of revenue and from the old ways of doing business. When we don't change, even satisfied customers may leave us when they can do business in a manner that is better for them.

All stakeholders may be important, but nobody said they were all equal. A hierarchy of different stakeholders exists, and Chapter 5 starts at the top of that hierarchy: customer relationships. We all need to move beyond customer satisfaction and achieve "true loyalty" from customers, where they willingly continue doing business with us. Survey evidence strongly indicates a general need to deepen our customer relationships beyond where they are today or risk losing them to competitors.

The need for stronger customer relationships is a constant challenge, but our ability to communicate with buyers and the potential for getting feedback from them has never been better. If children today correspond more with their friends than we ever did because of the wonders of the Web, then why shouldn't businesses achieve the same with their customers? With today's online technology, our communication with customers can be more frequent and hopefully more transparent. There are new ways to measure customer loyalty and evaluate business relationships. Online systems can also disseminate customer feedback throughout multinational organizations.

The Rise of Employees

If the status of customers places them first among the most important stakeholder segments, then the employee must be next, and fast growing in importance. In Chapter 6 and again at the end of the book, we make the point that employee relationships may offer businesses their best tactical opportunity in the realm of stakeholder strategy. With the economy booming and labor shortages looming, managers must definitely think of the care and nurturing of their employees as never before. New realities have in fact led to a different kind of contract with employees than existed a decade ago. Employee loyalty to any firm is now precarious. Examples are abundant of how, from a small company to a prominent multinational organization, leaders have effectively adjusted to the new realities of employee commitment.

Labor issues are becoming an economic version of the event depicted in the movie *The Perfect Storm,* in which a convergence of key forces becomes a weather crescendo. At the same time, some economists are predicting a "long boom" in sustained economic growth and demographers have indicated that the growth in the labor supply in the United States and in other countries is expected to slow considerably in the early twenty-first century. Compounding the looming labor shortage is the need for new and different skill sets related to information and communication technologies. And then throw into the mix the reality that the nature of the contract between workers and employers has changed in the United States and elsewhere in a post-downsizing era. The coming shortage will be more of skills than of warm bodies.

In addition to finding, attracting, and training skilled workers in the future, businesses face the ongoing challenge of keeping them. With the old bonds between employer and worker weakened, training serves a role beyond just honing the skills of workers. It may help them stay committed to your firm rather than leaving sooner to build their skills somewhere else. The true costs of employee turnover tend to be dramatically underestimated or ignored.

The new conceptual contract between worker and employer has been referred to as the "new deal." Louis Csoka, Research Director on Organizational Effectiveness with the Conference Board, says that the "re" words—reengineering and restructuring—have undermined the "i" words—information and involvement. Reengineering and restructuring have created an atmosphere of mistrust and a lack of commitment and loyalty from employees at the same time that the workforce requires individual involvement and information-sharing skills as never before.[6] The new deal recognizes the greater independence of workers, a more "conscious loyalty" versus blind loyalty, and the need to match new skills with the demands of the knowledge workplace and the global economy.[7]

Flexibility is key in the new workplace, along with mutual responsibility and respect. The implications for employers include shedding the paternal mind-set and forming something more like partnerships with employees—in short, treating them as stakeholders in a shared enterprise. *Fortune* magazine, in the January 2000 issue on the *100 Best Companies to Work For,* reports that skilled associates today command more input to senior management, more training, more flexibility in scheduling, and more access to the stock-purchase/options/awards programs than ever before.[8] Never has it been more crucial to understand our employees, not only by ensuring two-way communication, but by assessing employee loyalty as well. Chapter 6 explores the dynamics of employee loyalty as a business metric and a strategic goal.

Managing the Environment Is About Stakeholders' Interests, Too

Sustainability is a word that describes the total responsibilities of businesses today. It has been most frequently applied to environmental responsibilities: business growth and development accomplished in a way that sustains natural resources. We don't discuss environmentalism at length in this book, but stakeholder-oriented companies act on their principles of sustainability. Arthur Blank, co-founder and CEO of the Home Depot, announced in August 1999 one of the more dramatic voluntary policies of any major corporation regarding environmental protection: "Our pledge to our customers, associates and stockholders is that Home Depot will stop selling wood products from environmentally sensitive areas. Home Depot embraces its responsibility as a global leader to help protect endangered forests. By the end of 2002, we will eliminate from our stores wood from endangered areas . . . and give preference to 'certified' wood."[9]

This bold policy was all the more significant because of Home Depot's stature: The company happens to be the largest single worldwide lumber retailer. Category leaders tend to gain followers when they establish major new directions in policy, first from the members of the supply chain, and then, over time, even from competitors.

This stance is also remarkable because one of Home Depot's chief competencies is reinventing their supply chain and otherwise effectively managing costs. Buying certified wood commits the company to using only material that has been tracked from forest through manufacturing and distribution to ensure that sound environmental and social processes were used. Such a business decision follows an even higher principle than that of diligent cost management. Also interesting to note is that CEO Blank directed the pledge not only to customers (and the general public) but also to associates and stockholders; in other words, he tapped into the needs and desires of various stakeholders.

Win Swenson, a prominent corporate ethics attorney and prior National Managing Director of KPMG's Integrity Management Services, also views sustainability as a commitment to stakeholders of the business: "A commitment to sustainability is broader, deeper, and of substantially greater strategic value to a company than merely reporting on environmental outcomes. One goal of a sustainability initiative is to realize long-term business benefits by building non-financial performance measures—issues key stakeholders care about—into business processes."[10]

The Business Watchdogs Will Remain Alive and Well

What will happen to the enterprises or industries in the twenty-first century that overlook the interests of stakeholders or otherwise fail to heed important principles such as sustainable development? Well, government influence may have waned in terms of controlling marketplace economics, but governments will be all the more alert to exercise their watchdog role over commercial enterprise.And there will be non-governmental organizations (NGOs) serving in oversight roles to contend with as well.

Even the more democratic governments will re-regulate in cases in which a private enterprise, global or otherwise, has failed to be fair or reasonable to people or groups in its commercial dealings. For example, on the heels of deregulating whole industries such as transportation and natural gas, the U.S. government passed the Americans with Disabilities Act of 1990. Businesses and industries were judged to have failed consistently to offer access and facilities to their handicapped customers, associates, and visitors, so the government (expressing the will of the people) set the specifications for parking spaces, entrances, and other facility configurations.

With the growth in global trade and the World Wide Web enabling communication, there will be other influential agencies providing standards, oversight, and support to the global economy. These have been classified NGOs, often international in scope, that seek to influence certain segments or practices of commercial institutions.A well-known example is Greenpeace International, which claims no national interests but seeks to hold enterprises and countries accountable to environmental standards.

Another organization widely recognized in the business community is the International Organization for Standardization (ISO), whose standards have become almost a byword in firms that trade internationally. ISO is not an acronym, but derives from the Greek term for "equal" or "standard."

ISO is a federation of national standards bodies in some 130 countries, which work together to develop international business standards. Its intent is to promote international trade as well as to help emerging technologies and developing countries enter the global arena by providing conditions for industry-wide standardization.

ISO may be best known for its framework of quality assurance and management, ISO 9000. But ISO has also helped standardize telephone and bank card formats, freight containers, paper sizes, and other major elements of worldwide commerce. Lack of compliance with ISO standards can definitely pose a barrier to entry for any firm hoping to export goods and services.

Another heavy hitter in this category of global watchdogs is the previously mentioned Organization for Economic Cooperation and Development (OECD), which describes itself as "a club of like-minded countries . . . membership limited only by a country's commitment to a market economy and a pluralistic economy."[11] OECD today pulls together 29 member countries, with inputs from others, to discuss and develop economic and social policies such as guidelines for fighting bribery and corruption in trade. OECD also is in the process of rolling out new guidelines for multinational business corporations.

Extending Stakeholderism
Outside the "Immediate Family"

Businesses depend on forging powerful relationships with what we would call "extended stakeholders," those individuals outside an organization beyond customers who are important to the business, such as suppliers, alliance partners, community leaders, the media, and the government. Some of these directly support the business as part of the sales or supply chain of distribution, whereas others create or support our corporate reputations. Extended stakeholder issues such as supplier chain dynamics and corporate reputation are discussed in Chapter 7.

One of the more interesting business relationships evolving today is that between companies and their suppliers. The pendulum in some industries has swung from long-standing, predictable relationships between suppliers and companies to companies becoming incredibly demanding and selective, yet also tending to award bigger contracts to fewer partners. Part of this comes from adopting the Japanese style of management, but credit must also be given to the impact of Wal-Mart, Home Depot, and others now dominating their business categories. In response to this, the suppliers are now consolidating and innovating their products and services, fighting back with leverage of their own. The wise business leader rises above such a seesaw battle to maintain strong, lasting relationships with suppliers and alliance partners. Cisco Systems goes a step further with its strategy of creating happy acquisitions (otherwise almost an oxymoron in recent business history).

Aside from assuring regulatory or ethical compliance and competitiveness in one's "value chain" to the marketplace, outside stakeholder trust must be earned for another reason—maintaining one's good corporate reputation. The keepers of the flame of our reputations reside in these outside audiences—the general public, media, community leaders, and so forth. With ready accessibility to information about our firms, how our decisions are made, and the way our people are treated, corporate reputations are more fragile than ever. Business leaders need better ways to measure and manage their reputations, which are discussed in Chapter 7.

Business Outreach

Beyond helping protect their corporate reputations by maintaining relationships with important outside stakeholders, some firms become well known for generosity to their communities and/or to other meaningful causes. One of the themes discussed at length in Chapter 8 is the privilege of performing well enough as a commercial organization to enable charitable giving and employee volunteerism. Business people have unique talents to offer society that go beyond the creation of a strong economy. By temperament and profession, we are problem-solvers, and there are always social ills to be addressed.

Many stakeholders find that their association with an organization becomes more meaningful when the company gives back to others out of the fruits of its success. There are tools that can help justify the social investments a commercial firm makes, and there are potential alliances with specific causes that "fit" your organization. One of the most common examples (among several discussed in this chapter) is a local firm simply undertaking a United Way campaign. Because employees can personally relate to the various causes supported in their own communities, they feel part of a team that gives something back.

More than Principle—A System of Managing Loyalties

We wrap up in Chapter 9 by discussing the integration of relationships with different stakeholders. A payoff from attaining success in any stakeholder segment is that people always talk to others about the businesses they work with. Now those voices are louder. They are louder because technology has expanded the everyday communications network, and they are louder because constituents have more choices about companies they want to buy from, invest in, or be employed by. If we have been listening, then we know that people complain, recommend products, make referrals for jobs, and generally talk about companies as never before.

We present a template and some tools that are helping companies manage their stakeholder-focused corporations. A holistic approach to tracking our various constituent relationships requires a certain level of sophistication. Business has always been about people, but multiple-relationship management requires system thinking and application. Stakeholder commitment goals mean a balancing act, not only between your different types of stakeholders but also between running the business profitably in the short run and meeting the ultimate needs of constituents, including employees and customers. The ideal sequence starts by understanding your market value and the costs of the business operation well. That rewards us with the chance to enhance and build up these other relationships inside and outside the organization, to fuel continued growth.

All in the Balance

Balancing stakeholder needs does not mean turning one's back on the fiduciary obligations to shareholders, nor is it even about giving exactly equal weight to various shareholder types. As will be said more than once in this book, certain demands of capital (namely, running a profitable business) have to be addressed as a minimal requirement.

The twenty-first century will be an age of the "people assets" traditionally left out of financial reports: knowledge sharing and employee retention, customer loyalty, investor appeal, community support, and integrity "self-regulation." In reporting their assets, businesses will highlight their knowledge of their constituents. More significantly, the people assets will be targeted in the most basic strategies of the business, for innovation, communications, marketing, and corporate brand and reputation enhancement. Monetary and tangible goals will be set as always, but it will be the reputation influencers—buyers, alliance partners, employees, and investors—who will be targeted and accommodated in the twenty-first century as "the giants" of the new business era.

....

Case in Point: Cisco Systems—Connected with Stakeholders

The origin of Cisco Systems has become, as they say, the stuff of legends. Two graduate students at Stanford University, Leonard Bosak of the Computer Sciences School and Sandra Lerner of the Business School, joined a bootleg team constructing one of the first routers to connect the computer systems between different schools at Stanford. As they worked to develop this technology, Bosak and Lerner saw the commercial potential. They posed their ideas to the officials of Stanford but, refused resources and support, they left school and, with the help of capital raised from personal credit cards and the refinancing of their home, began Cisco Systems. The first task of the business was to develop a commercial network router for universities, aerospace companies, and the government; it was accomplished with team members including engineering friends from Stanford. Following Bosak's lead, the technicians frequently worked 100 or more hours a week. Within about two years, in 1986, they sold their first network router and by that time the market demand was insatiable. Not only had computers become widely used, but organizations were desperately seeking a means of connecting them into a network. In addition, a whole new realm was opening up apart from the target industries: Corporations of all types were increasingly converting from mini-computers to PCs, which innately required networking support.

According to *Hoover's,* Cisco sales were just $1.5 million in 1987 and ramped up to $28 million by 1989. An influx of capital and outside management expertise was sought at that time to stay ahead of the competition. Legendary was the keen insight of Donald Valentine of Sequoia Capital, who, unlike the many venture capitalists who turned down the opportunity, spent $2.5 million to buy a controlling stake and became chairman of Cisco.

Valentine brought in John Morgridge from laptop maker Grid Systems to be CEO, and the company went public in 1990. Operating under a more professional management style, the destiny of the original entrepreneurs was perhaps inevitable; the extremely outspoken Lerner, in particular, was anathema to the rest of the executive staff that Morgridge assembled. She was let go in 1990, with Bosak following shortly thereafter. The couple then sold all their stock back to the company for $170 million and soon gave most of it away to their favorite causes.

Through this level of charitable giving Lerner and Bosak certainly walked their talk and set a standard for Cisco, on which the company now seems refocused. The other legacies of Lerner and Bosak, aside from their sheer diligence and focus on technical innovation, were obviously understanding and adapting to customer needs and establishing a work culture that uniquely valued the employees.

From the very earliest days of making closing sales of their first products, the founders never just sold their routers as is. Customers were allowed to tinker with the systems that they purchased and often helped invent new features that were then built into the systems sold to other customers. This established a culture at Cisco Systems that emphasized flexibility in adapting to the needs of customers as well as learning from those experiences and offering better solutions for others. Lerner was said to have taken this to an extreme, never saying no to any request (leading to her downfall), but the notion of focusing on honoring customer input has remained a priority, during the Morgridge years of leadership through the early 1990s and in turn by current CEO John Chambers. The degree to which Cisco Systems embraces an orientation to customer needs is confirmed by the following points:

- Beyond the customization of products and solutions for individual customers, their corporate and marketing strategies and product designs have always been based on new learning from customers—ways that customers use their routers that were unexpected by Cisco.
- From the earliest days, Cisco communicated via the customers' preferred medium, technology. The company made early use of e-mail and the Internet with those they were working with on the customer side, who typically were technologists. By 1989 Cisco established one of the first online customer support sites and soon after an online database for reporting bugs in the systems. By 1993 they had established an Internet customer service hotline. Even earlier, Lerner and Bosak pioneered e-mail marketing (forerunner of SPAM) to the technologists in university settings.
- Morgridge and CEO John Chambers have operated from a fear that with its growth Cisco would distance itself from the needs of the customer. To counter that, selling and servicing occurs at different levels with various customers. Relationships are established not only with the decision-makers but also in the "bowels" of an organization. At all levels there is a dramatic focus on maintaining high levels of customer satisfaction.

- Using customer surveys to measure customers' assessment of
  their relationships with Cisco began in the early 1990s and
  continues today. In 1994 65 percent of all key customers
  were completely satisfied. When management decided to tie
  one-third of all employee bonuses to higher customer
  satisfaction, that score rose to 86 percent of customers fully
  satisfied. Chambers, whose early career was with IBM,
  constantly challenges the organization to never assume that
  they know more than the customer.

If rule number one at Cisco is to satisfy the customer, then rule
number two is concern for the employee. Aside from his IBM experience, which taught him to never be arrogant about customer
needs, John Chambers had an epiphany at Wang Laboratories,
where he presided over the release of thousands of employees
when the business fell out of sync with the changing marketplace:
He never again wants to lay off an employee and strives to deploy a
growth strategy that will avoid that necessity.

But the emphasis on understanding and accommodating employee needs goes far beyond avoiding layoffs. For one thing, Cisco
has established remarkably few layers of management for the size
of the organization. Decentralized among product groups and func-
tions, people generally are more involved in major decision making
and feel a sense of greater independence.

The culture at Cisco encourages people to feel comfortable ad-
mitting mistakes to management. Punishment comes only from not
learning from mistakes rather than from making them in the first
place. Individual uniqueness is encouraged, but in terms of style,
not ego. Innovation and productivity are rewarded, as opposed to
impressing a superior at the detriment of anyone else in the organization.

In terms of pay, it is interesting that Cisco's base salaries are noticeably lower than the industry average; apparently that deficit is
more than countered by bonuses and stock options in addition to
the unique culture. One recent estimate placed up to 20 percent of
the Cisco employees as having individual wealth of at least $1 mil-
lion. Although base pay has been assessed at 60 percent below

what could be made elsewhere for the same type of job, Cisco consistently achieves a lower employee turnover rate.

Employees have remarkable access to top management, and there is in general a spirit of open communication in the company. John Chambers as CEO holds regular breakfast meetings with employees at all levels, and questions can be asked on virtually any topic. Cisco's remarkable intranet system, one of the first in any corporation and still one of the most impressive in scope and quality, helps maintain a high sense of community across an increasingly huge corporation. Departments have their own sites for communicating events, changes, customer problems, and so forth. There are also sites that are accessible to sales forces, customers, and partners in all Cisco locations.

To fully understand the depth of employee focus within the culture at Cisco, we must consider what happens to the employees added by acquisition. Acquisitions have long been an integral part of Cisco's strategy for growth, but they posed a problem, because in the case of other firms, the company being acquired may lose as many as 40 percent of its employees during and after the merger. In contrast, Cisco's acquired employees have a higher rate of remaining with the company than even the existing Cisco employees. This remarkable record stems back to a few key principles related to acquired employees:

- The company applies the "Mario" rule—that no individual acquired with the merger will be let go without mutual consent—named after a key executive from one of the first Cisco acquisitions.
- Acquirees love the stock option plan at Cisco.
- Acquirees look forward to working in Cisco's famous culture of entrepreneurship and meaningful-work-without-so-much-politics.
- Not every employee ultimately is a fit for his or her job at Cisco, but there is to be fairness in any separations, meaning that even if there isn't total job security, at least every employee who leaves the company for any reason does so with dignity and financial fairness at the point of separation.

- Where acquisitions often fail because of the clash of different cultures or "personality conflicts," maverick-type personalities are allowed to flourish at Cisco as long as they otherwise meet basic principles related to teamwork, focusing on the customer, and so forth.

Even during the job-hunting phase, many individuals discover creativity and warmth in the way Cisco appeals to them as prospective employees. (Of course this is an organization seeking to hire up to a thousand employees a year, an incentive to get creative!) Individuals working with competitors who browse the Cisco home page find that they are immediately offered a screen asking them to apply to Cisco and explaining the corresponding benefits of becoming a member of the Cisco family.

Cisco's most impressive investments in community support or charity have been in the educational arena. Education offers the immediate benefit of increasing the supply of skilled labor, but Cisco has shown leadership in creating different levels of technical certification for the industry. This certification program, with its required course work offered by Cisco, has become a profit center for the organization.

Although the level of giving may never again be as high as that of Cisco's founders, the momentum for new giving built throughout the late 1990s. One of the first major grants was a program called "Virtual Schoolhouse," designed to enable school networking, established in 1996.

In the following year a general Cisco foundation was created, with the goal of making people more self-sufficient and productive in their lives. Grants to date range from supporting shelters and soup kitchens to more broad-based education and healthcare organizations. There is a matching grant program to motivate employee giving and support causes within the greater metropolitan areas of Cisco locations.

In 1999 a new program was unveiled by Chambers called Net Aid, which underwrote the simultaneous broadcasting of major rock concerts and supposedly reached the largest listening audience in history. It also provided an online clearinghouse for people to donate money or volunteer commitments to programs combating major global issues such as hunger and environmental problems.

Cisco keeps its strategy lean and clear: growth through high customer value in its markets, enabled by acquiring and retaining top talent. Growth, of course, thrills investors (including employees) because of the corresponding stock value growth and underwrites the ability to give back to worthy causes, which seems to make everybody even happier. This is in many ways the prototype of taking a stakeholder focus and reaping the benefits.

....

Value in the Eye of the Beholder

The thread that runs through all the new era implications of doing business in the twenty-first century is that we must earn people's commitment and loyalty. Businesses have a huge stake in retaining relationships with investors, employees, customers, regulators, and others. The stakeholders have become giants because they have leverage as never before. The value they see in associating with one business versus another will be based on how well the business has earned their commitment and how well-burnished and protected the company's reputation is.

We have described the components of a stakeholder information model that integrates the feedback from all of your key constituents. Because value is only in the eye of the beholder, the only way for businesses to know their value will be to determine exactly who their stakeholders are . . . and to ask them. The urgency to adapt to stakeholder power and leverage it as a business strategy is not just a business fad, it is a winning approach and the more satisfying way to do business.

2

Power to the People

A fair question to ask at this point is, "Who exactly are these stakeholders, and why are they really so important to business strategy and success?" If that question has crossed your mind, you are not alone. In fact, try playing a word association game with a typical businessperson. Say the word "business" and what will you hear first? Chances are it won't be "people" or "relationships." Instead you may hear "profits," "management," "dot-com," or "stock market" because business still tends to be associated mainly with money and performance. However, in the new economy driven by knowledge assets and technology with evolving channels of goods and services, the leading business organizations are already beginning to focus on *people* more than on the traditional elements and indicators of business success.

Doing Business with People

Think about what money represents to anyone who believes that business is just about making money. Money measures the value of-

23

fered someone for goods or services. Commerce, then, is people giving something of value to other people; money simply enables the
process. Before money existed, we know that people bartered to get
what they wanted, and bartering is still used exclusively in some cultures and in certain situations in most cultures.

So *people* have arguably always been the most important ingredi-
ent in business. This may be why people in their various business
roles are increasingly referred to as the "stakeholders" of the enterprise. Business has its greatest stake in people—sellers and buyers to
be sure, but a cast of individuals in other roles as well.

What Are Stakeholders?

Stakeholder is a term for individuals or groups who have a connection to or an association with an organization. They have a stake,
claim, or vested interest in the day-to-day operation of the business.
The relationship is nearly always reciprocal, where the business has
some stake in the individuals or groups as well, needing their resources or their influence in running the business. Beyond the owners or shareholders of an enterprise, stakeholders always include
customers and employees. They may also, depending on the organization and its mission and function, include suppliers, lenders, alliance
partners, local communities, political/advocacy groups or opinion
leaders, and government agencies.

Knowledge and Awareness of Stakeholders

Based on a 1998 international study on the topic by Walker Information, three of every four executives in North America are familiar with
the term *stakeholder,* but just 52 percent of them in the United States
(78 percent in Canada) actually use the term.[1] The groups most recognized as being stakeholders were employees, customers, and shareholders. In fact, executives' beliefs about who stakeholders are tend
to be pretty narrow. Even with prompting, a majority of respondents
did not recognize certain constituents—financial analysts (50 per-

cent), government/agencies (40 percent), and the community (only 26 percent)—as being stakeholders. These data suggest that some business leaders are underestimating the importance of these constituencies to their business.

In the United States, more executives thought of investors/owners as stakeholders than the number who put customers in that category. "Having a stake" in a company makes us think of financially investing in an enterprise, having a vested desire to see it perform, and wanting a say in how it operates. Owners or investors, although certainly qualifying as stakeholders, represent a particular type of stakeholder most typically known as shareholders. And shareholders are often sharply distinguished from other stakeholders in terms of their beliefs about where the business should focus: on creating value exclusively for the shareholders or on creating value for various other stakeholders as well.

Shareholder Value Versus Stakeholder Value

Business advisors and economists have been arguing over this issue for some time. In the late 1980s and early 1990s, with the increase in merger and reengineering activity, there seemed to be more vocal shareholder value practitioners, with occasional backlash from stakeholder advocates.

The proponents of shareholder value stand on a principle perhaps as old as commerce itself and exemplified in the words of Nobel Prize–winning economist Milton Friedman: "There is one and only social responsibility of business . . . to increase its profits, so long as it stays within the rules of the game."[2] Friedman and other proponents of shareholder value argue that focusing beyond what is of ultimate value to the owners of businesses will dilute business focus, reward inefficiency and waste, and generally not give due diligence to the expectations of shareholders. Businesses adhering to this philosophy naturally focus on metrics such as revenue growth, earnings, economic value added (EVA), market capitalization, and shareholder return.

Not all financial measures are considered to be equal, and there has been steadily increasing emphasis on the stock price and market capitalization. In *The New Corporate Cultures*, Allan Kennedy and Terrence Deal locate the turning point in the late 1970s, when Alfred Rappaport, an accounting professor at Northwestern University's graduate business school, made an effective case for using cash-flow analysis to assess the value of a business enterprise.[3] Rappaport pointed out that traditional measures such as return on investment and earnings per share were less accurate than cash-flow analysis because only cash-flow analysis estimated the return to the investor in the form of dividends and increased stock value over time. As Deal and Kennedy concluded, "Cash flow analysis not only was a better predictor of the value of a business enterprise, but also could forecast future stock market price levels more accurately. Thus, the notion of shareholder value was born."[4]

Among the early "adopters" of cash-flow analysis were investment bankers in the 1970s and 1980s. They saw the opportunity of creating tremendous positive cash flow for themselves and other investors by gaining control of firms where sizable cost reductions could be made and/or assets such as business units or subsidiaries could be profitably split off and sold.

Certain individuals, notably Jerome Kohlberg and George Roberts, who ultimately formed KKR with Henry Kravis, developed a technique that became known as leveraged buyout (LBO). They put together acquisition deals that promised investors a large enough return to warrant assessing healthy fees on top of their 20 percent cut of any investment gains. In keeping with the definition of *leverage,* the deals were made with only a small portion of investor equity, combined with massive credit obtained from financial institutions.

By the mid-1980s, what to that point had been mainly mutually agreed-to, "friendly" acquisitions led to decidedly unfriendly ones, and the era of "hostile takeovers" had begun. Facing this threat, boards and senior management were compelled to focus more exclusively on ways to assess and bolster shareholder value. Stock options inevitably came into vogue as the preferred approach to compensate senior managers in a way that focused on earnings and growth, the engines of the stock value. As Deal and Kennedy put it, "Old methods for measuring progress (had) to be jettisoned. When managerial pay practices changed to make sure managers heeded these new priorities, the future was determined."[5]

And what did this future bring? For one thing, the total compensation for senior executives of the largest corporations began to skyrocket in the 1990s. Deal and Kennedy examined this trend by recording the largest U.S. pay package per year. Top compensation hovered around $1 million in the mid-1970s; from 1981 through 1990, it was in eight figures (more than $10 million). From 1990 through 1997 the highest-paid executives exceeded $100 million on five occasions. Sandy Weill topped that record by earning $230.7 million at Travelers in 1997.[6]

Executives being paid largely in stock options naturally focused on the primary elements that drive shareholder value, notably sales and earnings growth. As proven by the corporate raiders, one of the fastest means of raising stock value is to boost profits by cutting costs. This ushered in the era of "crash dieting" by large companies, also known as *reengineering* or *downsizing*.

Although downsizing may be absolutely necessary in a crisis or to deal with what has clearly become an overstaffed or outdated company, there have been too many cases of cutting expenses (jobs/people) suddenly and dramatically, primarily because the corporate focus was fixed so exclusively on boosting value for shareholders. It seems fair to question a system that essentially rewards management for eliminating people's jobs, and the evidence is hard to refute. Deal and Kennedy merely summarized what business news and journals had already reported: that leaders of firms cutting thousands of employees were simultaneously being compensated with more than $10 million.

Shareholder Value Personified

Carried to the extreme, a shareholder focus counters the belief that businesses have obligations to people other than the executives and owners. For example, Scott Paper, under the charge of "Chainsaw Al" Dunlap, cut 11,000 jobs, dropped virtually all contributions to its local communities to the tune of nearly $4 million, cut all employee memberships in industry organizations, and wiped out direct sponsorship of trade events.[7]

At the time, Wall Street and major shareholders applauded these moves. With the stock price moving up dramatically in the short run, Dunlap became very wealthy himself because the company was soon sold off. But at least one business journalist, John Byrne of *Business-Week,* detected a dark side to the events at the time, claiming that Dunlap "cut plenty of muscle along with the fat . . . is leaving the company in a much less healthy position than he claims . . . and claims responsibility for (new products that) are the result of years of effort by ousted staffers."[8]

Dunlap reappeared at Sunbeam, where he cut 6,000 jobs. But this time he lost favor on Wall Street because the stock continued to languish. He also lost credibility with his board, and the company ultimately attracted the attention of regulators. John Byrne later chronicled Dunlap's fall from grace at Sunbeam followed by the review of the company's accounting practices in his 1999 book *Chainsaw.*[9]

There is no question that Al Dunlap made news because he was extreme in his shareholder advocacy. But why were so many other business leaders caught up in downsizing and reengineering at the time? One answer we've addressed is the desire for short-term earnings or profit stemming from the cost savings. To endure, however, sales revenue streams must continue despite the staff cutbacks. Business leaders also believed that dramatic cost cutting helped set the stage for a company to grow. But a study of corporate growth dispels this notion. Of the profitable, growing firms in the Fortune 1,000 from 1988 to 1993, only 7 percent had been cost cutters during the previous five-year period. As the authors of the study, Dwight L. Gertz and Joao P.A. Baptista of Mercer Management Consulting, concluded in their book, "No company ever shrank to greatness."[10]

Perhaps the "elephant in the living room" concerning extreme shareholder advocacy is the ethics involved. Michael Rion, a noted business ethics consultant with an industrial management background, makes the argument that "to say that managers should simply maximize profits as agents of shareholders assumes that the market dynamics are always effective and relatively quick to respond. [Since the market doesn't always work that way], . . . corporate emphasis on production goals, marketing efforts, and profitability can lead to such problems as unsafe products, environmental pollution, and economic hardship and uncertainty in plant communities facing a shutdown."[11]

Business executives and managers naturally want simple guidelines for decision making, but fixing exclusively on the notion of maximizing market value is apparently not a sound one nor an ethical guide. Running a business strictly to enhance stock value appears to undermine keeping commitments to other people important to the business and ultimately fails as a long-term performance strategy.

Giving Credence to Stakeholders

In contrast to the shareholder value theory, companies advocating a stakeholder value approach believe in considering the day-to-day priorities of multiple constituents. Supporting stakeholder value means reasonably balancing priorities across the interests of various stakeholders: shareholders, customers, employees, suppliers/alliance partners, the community, opinion leaders, and others.

These companies normally have a mission statement and a set of core values that emphasize this philosophy. Usually, they see themselves as especially accountable to customers and to employees, who along with shareholders are the "highest among equals" of the various stakeholders. They see the need for good relationships with other stakeholder groups as well, which can vary depending on the business and the situation. In addition to the standard types of financial indicators, these firms also set goals for such metrics as customer satisfaction and employee loyalty.

Eastman Chemical, a large organization enabled to take a fresh look at its business after being spun off by Eastman Kodak Co. in 1994, was cited in *CFO Magazine* by Bill Birchard, former editor of *Enterprise* magazine, for its mission "to create superior value" for five stake- holder groups: customers, investors, employees, suppliers, and nearby communities. Management began to see how their decisions had an impact on various groups and became adept at choosing a course that helped most constituents. A management training course guided executives through online scenarios to teach the alignment between the stakeholders' interests and how to make balanced decisions.[12] Eastman Chemical's market performance was very strong until 1997. Since then, because capital had begun moving toward technology markets, Eastman's market value has leveled off. But the company has still outperformed others in its category.

Stakeholder theory has, of course, been criticized by shareholder theory advocates for "softening" the realities of running businesses that face competition in the global arena. They cite the innate con- flicts between stakeholder group priorities and say there will be con- fusion unless all decisions are seen through the lens of shareholder value. Another point condemning a stakeholder focus is the fiduciary obligation of management to manage capital effectively for the bene- fit of shareholders.

Excessive management salaries and benefits and lack of account- ability have been attributed to overlooking shareholder value, result- ing in waste and the businesses becoming vulnerable to hostile takeovers. Elaine Sternberg, a London-based business ethics and cor- porate governance consultant, told Birchard and *CFO Magazine*: "Stakeholder theory encourages arrogant and unresponsive manage- ments; extravagance in salaries, perks and premises, indulgence of in- ferior performance from employees and suppliers; resistance to takeover bids that would benefit shareholders; acceptance of takeover bids that would make little financial sense; . . . all sorts of waste and irresponsibility which translates into low profits and poor share performance over time."[13]

Meeting Somewhere in the Middle

The shareholder and stakeholder positions are not necessarily poles apart. An advocate for the owner/investor approach may be the first to admit that shareholder value will not be maximized for long if there is high employee dissatisfaction and turnover, or if there isn't high customer retention and growth of major accounts. "What we say is, if you continue to focus on creating shareholder value, and you develop a strategy to do that, then by definition all the other groups will get their appropriate treatment and respect," said Basil L. Anderson, CFO and professed shareholder advocate at Scott during the Dunlap era.[14]

Stakeholder advocates in turn tend to include the shareholders or owners at the top of the list of priorities, as seen in the profile of the dueling platforms in Table 2.1. In a sense, then, even stakeholder value believers give credit to the investor or owner as the "very first among equals" in the realm of constituents, or at least as the first threshold for accountability in business performance.[15]

Stakeholders Getting Their Due

Although most business leaders today likely embrace parts of both the investor and the stakeholder value arguments, the pendulum is definitely swinging toward considering stakeholders. Consider the legacy left by the Total Quality Management (TQM) movement and its Malcolm Baldrige Award, which resulted in an overdue focus on customer satisfaction and on simply providing excellent products and services. Another outcome of TQM and Japanese competition was the empowerment of workers to make decisions rather than wasting knowledge and experience within the old command-and-control cultures.

Or watch businesses scramble for top talent in a near-full economy today and consider the coming struggle to meet labor needs as baby boomers age and retire from the workforce. Think about the increased

TABLE 2.1   Dueling Platforms

	Shareholder Advocate	**Stakeholder Advocate**
Corporate Mission value	Maximize shareholder value	Maximize value for all stakeholders
Priority in Decisions	Shareholder interests	Shareholders, customers, employees
Accountability	To shareholders	To shareholders, customers, employees, suppliers, government, communities
Performance Measurements	Shareholder value: economic value-added, return on equity, total shareholder return, etc.	Shareholder value, as well as, at minimum, customer and employee satisfaction
Compensation	Tied to economic value creation	Tied to mix of economic value creation and stakeholder satisfaction

Source: Reprinted from Bill Birchard, "How Many Masters Can You Serve?" *CFO Magazine* (July 1995).

interdependence of firms within supply chains and the reliance on alliance partners for manufacturing, sales, and distribution. The priorities of partners and suppliers have never been more important.

Think of the growing concern about corporate reputations, evidenced by the various "most admired" rankings of firms. Even the demands of various local communities and the public have grown, with companies expected to be, at a minimum, safe places to work and environmentally friendly; ideally, they also will be sponsors of programs for community needs and related activities. Many investors now rely on funds and agencies that help them invest in firms with socially responsible policies and practices.

These examples signal a fundamental shift in business leaders' thinking about measuring success in terms of providing what people want instead of just looking at the bottom line. They are not forgetting that businesses must perform financially, but they are becoming convinced that stakeholder value is linked directly to the bottom line. In Walker's 1998 Stakeholder Awareness Study, 72 percent of North American executives collecting customer feedback were positive about its usefulness for business planning and change, and 78 percent used customer information frequently to forecast future business results.

Stakeholder Commitment Begets Shareholder Value

Value is created and maintained for business investors by and with good relationships with stakeholders. Evidence is building a case for stakeholder perspective being a means to shareholder fulfillment. In fact, at least two major studies have indicated a direct relationship between increasing value for stakeholders and the ensuing value that is built over time for investors.

One study was done by Harvard University's John P. Kotter and James L. Heskett in 1992 and reported in *Corporate Culture and Performance*.[16] They learned that the highest financial performance was achieved by companies that had built their cultures on the premise that customers and employees must be valued in addition to shareholders.

Kotter and Heskett studied performance over time between companies taking a more stakeholder-focused approach and those deploying a more traditional, bottom-line approach to management. The stakeholder-savvy group of firms averaged growth of 682 percent over an 11-year period, while the companies that were not stakeholder focused grew just 166 percent over the same period.

James Collins and Jerry Porras reported similar findings after examining long-term performance by leading companies; they detailed the results of their study in *Built to Last*. Over several decades, "visionary" firms that followed core values emphasizing specific stakeholder principles beyond just financial performance dramatically outperformed the stock market as a whole.[17]

Collins and Porras, whose study is discussed in greater detail in Chapter 3, on corporate integrity, also speak to the tension or balance between short-term financial performance (shareholder value) and responsibility to other stakeholders. They found that the stakeholder-oriented "visionary" companies disputed that there even was a dilemma. Instead of seeing different good outcomes as a win/lose trade-off, they found that people pushed each other to achieve both good outcomes. In other words, visionary companies believe they can satisfy investors with short-term performance *and* still effectively meet their obligations to customers, employees, and other stakeholders embodied in their core values.

The authors of the study illustrated this conclusion with F. Scott Fitzgerald's definition of high intelligence: "The test of a first-rate intelligence is the ability to hold two opposed ideas in the mind at the same time and still be able to function."[18] Based on performance over time alone, the visionary firms in this study confirmed their intelligence, and they did it by holding that people values and profit values are complementary goals, not contradictory ones.

Accounting for Stakeholders and Performance Measurement

Most companies have invested in measures for certain stakeholders. The Walker Information North American Study on Stakeholder Measurement found that about three in four U.S. executives (84 percent in Canada) say that their organizations gather customer and employee feedback through survey research.

By measuring feedback from constituents, executives and directors may be recognizing what has become apparent to a number of business analysts: A healthy portion of the value of a corporation does not show up on the balance sheet, and relationships with stakeholders are leading indicators of financial performance.

Ernst & Young, through its Center for Business Innovation, produced some interesting findings in a report called "Measures That Matter."[19] They reported that, on average, 35 percent of buy-side investment decisions are driven by nonfinancial data. For example, institutional investors consider the value of the organization to include assets that are harder to count than pure financial performance.

The "hidden capital" not on the balance sheet, according not only to Ernst & Young but to other experts as well, has several components that clearly include the relationships the firm has with key stakeholders. The ability to attract and retain talented staff was the fifth most valuable intangible factor in E & Y's study, ahead of market share, management experience, process quality, and other factors. Out of 39 factors, customer satisfaction levels ranked eleventh—a surprisingly low result in the minds of many, and an indicator that business leaders still have a long way to go in understanding the value of strong customer relationships to long-term performance.

The highest-ranking factors in the E & Y study were the quality of management and innovativeness. These factors also relate to corporate reputation, which, by definition, is viewed from the eyes of key stakeholders. For anyone still wondering how much reputation really matters, consider that the top 10 percent of *Fortune* magazine's "Most Admired" companies did twice as well as the market over a 13-year span.[20]

In contrast, it isn't difficult to guess what tends to happen after companies experience the publication of corporate crises, and that the cost of repairing a damaged reputation is high. A conclusive study by researcher Jeff Frooman of the University of Pittsburgh was published in *Business and Society Review* with the takeaway that "shareholder wealth decreases . . . when firms act in a socially irresponsible or illegal manner."[21] Some of the widely reported corporate disasters of a safety or environmental nature in recent years are obvious examples of how such problems can drive away stakeholders as well as investors for some time. But mistakes happen in even the best companies, and the ensuing publicity in a world equipped with CNN and the Internet can be painful.

Lockheed Martin Corporation is a leading aerospace and defense contracting company with a solid reputation (the only aerospace defense firm listed in *Computerworld* magazine in 2000 as one of its

"Top 100 Places to Work in Information Technology").[22] But between August 1998 and December 1999, the firm had three of its Titan rocket missions explode or send satellites into orbit incorrectly; the company also faced the failure of two Mars exploration missions.[23] In early 2000 there followed public accounts of alleged discrimination in a manufacturing plant and a rocket launch postponement.

During the same time period, the company's stock had headed south at the end of 1998; stayed down in 1999; but appeared to be rallying through the second quarter of 2000.

The *Denver Business Journal* article stated that the first priority for Louis R. Hughes, new President and COO, was to reestablish the company's *reputation*. If Lockheed's market value continues to improve after being down one year, the company may exemplify that although even good companies that make mistakes must take their lumps, they can withstand the subsequent damage to their reputations better than most, and make their comebacks.

Brand image is also part of reputation, and it also has powerful effects on shareholder value. The value of brands for the likes of the Coca-Cola Company and McDonald's has been estimated in the tens of billions of dollars.[24]

The Case for Nonfinancial Measures

There are pressures mounting from institutional investors and from the impact of regulation to begin disclosing certain nonfinancial measures to investors and others. Disclosure is admittedly a controversial issue, with opinions divided sharply over the wisdom of moving beyond traditional, auditable financials. The Securities and Exchange Commission's (SEC) "Safe Harbor" legislation of 1995 gave a clear example of how nonfinancial data are being recognized for their increased role in investor decisions.[25]

Formally called the Private Securities Litigation Reform Act, this legislation's intent is to encourage greater disclosure of forward-looking corporate performance information. Companies are otherwise naturally hesitant to report leading indications rather than just past performance, fearing potential liability from misleading anyone. The Safe Harbor legislation seeks to protect disclosure of such "soft" information. This legislation was supposed to encourage firms to disclose more than just financial data to help investors make better decisions. Although the results have been mixed, there is little question that it was a step toward broader disclosure, which could include information about stakeholder relationships.

The financial community also seems to be raising the bar in terms of wanting nonfinancial information. Active institutional investors such as the California Public Employees Retirement System are demanding access to such information because their investment strategy is long-term in nature. E & Y's study also confirmed that sell-side analysts make more accurate earnings forecasts when they use nonfinancial measures.[26] Because analysts are in the business of being accurate with their forecasts, we can expect that they will increasingly demand that type of nonfinancial information.

Beyond Measures, the Call for a New Approach to Accounting

A special report in *Fast Company* magazine's January/February 2000 issue emphasizes that traditional accounting systems are increasingly irrelevant.[27] The report by Alan Webber (founding editor of *Fast Company* and prior editorial director of *Harvard Business Review*) was heavily influenced by Baruch Lev, the Phillip Bards Professor of Accounting and Finance at New York University's Leonard N. Stern School of Business. Lev is also Director of the Vincent C. Ross Institute of Accounting Research and the Project for Research on Intangibles.

The article concludes that accounting systems today face a serious problem. They were constructed to provide hard data regarding the evaluation of assets in dollars and cents, profits, losses, and so forth. Yet the new economy is very much about value created by intangible assets such as ideas, brands, ways of working, and franchises. The question then becomes how to account for these intangibles.

The seriousness of this problem has been confirmed by the gyrations of technology stock values in the current market. Are biotech, technology, or other knowledge-based companies overvalued or undervalued? How exactly should we value such organizations? Lev maintains that these are the questions that cannot be completely answered by our current business accounting system, which dates back centuries to when transactions were in durable goods and assets could be easily accounted for:"Accounting [today], in other words, no longer delivers accountability."[28]

Giving further evidence for this notion, Weber cites the market-to-book ratio for the S&P 500, the largest companies in the United States, which are by no means purely focused on the "new economy." This ratio at year-end 1999 was greater than six, meaning that the number at the bottom of the asset balance sheet—the total measured assets for companies—represents just 15 percent of the actual market value.

There has actually been a trend for some time toward intangible assets representing an increasingly higher portion of the overall value of public companies. The Brookings Institute calculated that intangible assets across a range of U.S. manufacturing and mining companies rose from just 38 percent of market values in 1982 to 62 percent 10 years later.[29]

What exactly are intangible assets? Product innovation (talented people creating and launching new or improved products), assets associated with a company's brand (including the caliber of management and employees as well as products and services), structural assets or unique ways of doing business, and any monopoly or barrier to entry advantages are all intangible assets. Clearly, developing strong relationships with stakeholders can play an increasingly critical role in explaining the overall value of organizations today.

Figure 2.1 reflects the analysis of intangible assets for some individual firms by Jeremy Hope and Tony Hope, international business consultants and the co-authors of *Competing in the Third Wave*.[30] The data show that some companies and sectors may still have an abundance of tangible assets, for example, Ford and the auto industry. But

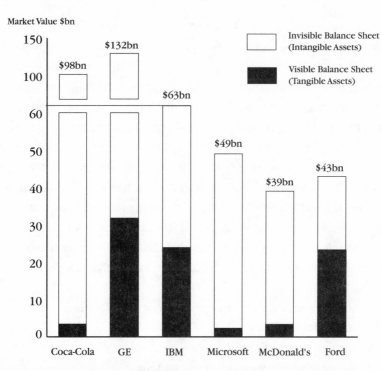

FIGURE 2.1   The Ratio of Intangible to Tangible Assets.
Source: Jeremy Hope and Tony Hope, *Competeing in the Third Wave* (Boston: Harvard Business School Press, 1997), 172.

for others, intangible assets are dominant. Examples of these companies are Microsoft, representing the new economy,   and Coca-Cola and McDonald's, "old" economy firms that continue to leverage their company brands and reputations in the marketplace.

To account for the impact of stakeholders and other intangible assets, Baruch Lev is working to revolutionize the measurement of such assets. He is trying to move beyond just accounting for past earnings and to credit the "knowledge earnings" of the organization. He gives this example of calculating the knowledge earnings:

Merck and Company, for instance, has lots of laboratories and manufacturing facilities. The equipment there is not unique. What is unique are the people, the patents, the knowledge that is being developed there. So when I subtract from the total normalized earnings a reasonable return

on the physical and financial assets, I define what remains as the knowledge earnings. Those are the earnings that are created by the knowledge assets.[31]

If we are on our way to a new calculation of the assets and performance of an organization, there is little question that there will be increased attention given to the specific measurement of the
relationships that companies have with their key stakeholders. The
caliber of goodwill with stakeholders is simply too critical an asset
not to be accounted for. The fact that measuring such assets is not as
easy or clear-cut as measuring tangible assets does not mean we
should not at least develop such metrics. Otherwise, how can leaders
know if they are achieving such common value goals as:

- Commitment and loyal intentions among strategic
  accounts/customers
- Commitment from employees
- Support from local community leaders
- Objective treatment by media
- Committed support from vendors and alliance partners

Balancing the Scorecard

Breakthrough work by the team of Robert S. Kaplan and David P. Norton addresses the same problem (what they term "the immovable ob-
ject of the historical—cost financial accounting model") by offering
an approach called the "balanced scorecard." This model not only provides a new approach to measurement that includes stakeholder and
other intangible assets and activities beyond the financials but is also
a catalyst for changing the organization to become more competitive.
Kaplan and Norton firmly believe that companies focusing on short-
term financial performance are trading off their future investment in
growth opportunities.[32]

Like Lev, Kaplan and Norton believe financial indicators provide historical information that is merely the outcome of other activities by the organization. The balanced scorecard approach broadens corporate financial measures to include indicators regarding customers, internal/business processes, and learning and growth. To them, two of the four broad categories of critical measures are directly related to stakeholders: *customers*, which includes measures of customer loyalty as well as drivers such as delivery time and satisfaction with product use, and *learning and growth*, which includes some measures of employee talent and skill levels along with retention and satisfaction data about key employees and the training and information-sharing processes within the organization. Table 2.2 lists the balanced scorecard components.

The balanced scorecard is certainly an elegant business measurement model, and it has been adopted by hundreds of companies in one form or another. Some of our clients and other companies we

TABLE 2.2　The Balanced Scorecard

Financial Perspective	Customer Perspective	Internal Business Process Perspective	Learning and Growth Perspective
Performance related to strategic financial goals	Performance related to strategic customer loyalty and perceived value	Performance in processes most critical to achieving financial and customer perspectives	Performance in developing employees, information systems and organizational incentives that support the other perspectives

Source: Adapted from Robert S. Kaplan and David P. Norton, *The Balanced Scorecard* (Boston: Harvard Business School, 1996).

meet at conferences using this approach have modified it to create a fifth formal category of measures related to employees in addition to the learning and knowledge management/measurement. This step recognizes employees for their critical value to companies and forces leaders to establish specific goals related to the retention, equipping, and managing of employees.

However, Kaplan and Norton and many practitioners of balanced scorecard measures appear to have overlooked the important category of tracking other stakeholder groups, perhaps because (unlike the universal customer and employee constituents) different constituencies are critical to different firms. The strong companies of the future will develop key business indicators for each stakeholder group that is critical to its success, as regulators are to healthcare systems today or as community leaders are to many organizations that have expressed commitments to supporting local communities that in turn provide a living environment for workers, education, and tax and other regulations.

•••

Case in Point

Sir Iain Vallance, chairman of British Telecommunications, needed no convincing as his firm embarked on an explicit upgrading of ethics in 1996. "Those of us who manage companies have a responsibility to underline the importance of ethics to our enterprises," he says. "There can be no question of simply paying lip service to the idea. We must, in our actions as well as our words, show our employees, our customers, and, indeed, all our stakeholders what our company stands for and what are our values."[33]

Among his moves in following up on that philosophy, Vallance issued in 1999 a report on BT's progress in dealing with each BT stakeholder: shareholders, customers, employees, and communities. The report details BT's programs to improve its performance. It also reveals sensitive measures of success. As just one example, shareholders learned that in 1996 only 64 percent of those attending the annual meeting felt that the question-and-answer session was open and honest. In 1998, 77 percent felt that the session was open and honest.[34]

The business of British Telecommunications is communications; telephone, data networks, Internet and media, private networks and solutions, mobile communications, and customer and operator assistance are the services they provide. For their fiscal year ended in March 1999, BT had 18 billion pounds in turnover (roughly $27 billion U.S. revenue).

Not surprisingly, BT's mission ties their financial objectives to stakeholder responsibilities. The ultimate goal—"to generate shareholder value by seizing opportunities in the communications market world-wide"—is to be achieved "while playing our part in the community and achieving the highest standards of integrity, customer satisfaction, and employee motivation."[35]

In leading his company to higher performance and new reporting on stakeholder satisfaction, Vallance recognized what the analyses of business ethics by Walker Information studies have borne out. Three factors above all affect peoples' perceptions of the ethical high ground of a company: the perceived integrity of senior leaders, the commitment to integrity communicated by those leaders, and the consistent demonstration by those leaders of ethical values to all stakeholders in all situations. Vallance has gone further than many leaders, exemplifying integrity by publishing such a revealing report focusing on BT's relationships with stakeholders.

Many Roads Pointing Toward Stakeholder Measurement

We see some signs that customer satisfaction, employee motivation, and community involvement are becoming integral parts of corporate mission and strategy in more and more organizations. Not every CEO may share the view of BT's Vallance that meeting such goals is a matter of principle or ethics. But we hope to convince any business leader that winning commitment from key constituents drives the other major business goals. And increasingly, we will all be competing with businesses that have learned the principles of good business-to-people relationships with stakeholders. Changes in accounting systems to embody intangible assets, measure knowledge assets in particular, and flesh out a balanced scorecard that includes stakeholder measures are all changes virtually ensuring that leading organizations will be more effectively tracking the relationships they have with key stakeholders.

In the next chapter we examine approaches to better understanding these constituent relationships by addressing questions such as

- Who are our most important constituents or stakeholders?
- Is there a way to categorize the depth of commitment that someone (a customer, an employee, etc.) has to our business?
- What are some of the steps to enhance people's commitment to our business?

Harnessing the Power

Stakeholder Loyalty

Let us First Commit to Commit. . .

Like major cities, large organizations or institutions do not exactly have reputations for being "user-friendly," or sensitive to the needs of their constituents. Politicians have been known to seize upon this reality when they rail about "big corporations," "big pharmaceutical firms," "big government," or simply "Washington."

Considering the very nature of large companies reveals some understanding about the generalizations about bigness. As they grow larger and more complex, organizations inevitably create distance between position levels and between departments within the company, not to mention between many of those within the institution and constituents on the outside.

As a result, the more successful large firms work hard to counter this tendency. They create core values stating that constituents will be of paramount importance, then they back up those claims with structure and accountability. If the core value is, "The customer is number one," or "We care about our employees," then the leadership has committed to invest resources toward building those relationships and earning in return a commitment from those stakeholders. We agree with Iain Vallance of British Telecommunications about the principle involved here: that businesses have obligations to people and to maintaining good business relationships. No one ever questions being obliged to owners or shareholders in business; likewise, there should be no question about obligations to other stakeholders, either.

Making the expected profit for the owners is building a relationship because it meets an obligation: They made the investment expecting a certain return, and fulfilling that commitment only strengthens the relationship. We forget that virtually every aspect of business is really about relationships. We make "virtual contracts" at every point of sale—the customer pays for a product or service, and the company is expected to deliver something of value and in accordance with expectations. We recruit and employ someone with the right skill and experience, who comes to work for us as an employee or a supplier; we pay these individuals for their services and ensure they are reasonably equipped and facilitated in their work. That reciprocity is once again mutual commitment and relationship.

Even civic and government leaders define their relationships with business leaders by making commitments, when they work alongside each other to find equity for civic projects and when tax breaks and other incentives are invested to attract commercial enterprises.

As we have already shown, the global economy of the twenty-first century will experience shortages of skilled labor and increased competitive pressures, so learning how to manage business relationships has never been more important. Stakeholder relationship management has become a focal point for business success, and world-class leaders recognize this reality. *Industry Week* announced its fourth annual list of the world's 100 Best Managed Companies by concluding that these companies "not only consistently demonstrate an ability to grow sales and profits; they also invest in their employees, new technologies, the environment, safety, and their local communities."[1]In short, the companies best poised to succeed are meeting commitments to people who are important to them—and these people are more than just the investors and the board.

In 1998, the Foundation for the Malcolm Baldrige National Quality Award sponsored a study of large-company CEOs asking about the major trends affecting U.S. companies and the ability of the companies and their CEOs to deal effectively with those changes. Fifty percent of the respondents believed that most CEOs need "a great deal" of improvement in their ability to "work well with different stakeholders." In addition, some stakeholder relationships are becoming more critical while others are becoming less so. More than 75 percent of the CEOs view focusing on customers and employees as becoming more important than ever, and more than six in ten believe certain other stakeholders are becoming more critical as well: suppliers (67 percent), outside board directors (63 percent), and institutional shareholders (61 percent). On the other hand, seven in ten CEOs think that labor unions are becoming *less* important stakeholders, and nearly half feel the same way about individual (as opposed to institutional) investors.[2]Indeed, the 2000 Baldridge criteria themselves reflect the increasing urgency to manage stakeholder relationships, allocating 345 of the 1,000 evaluation points to themes that relate directly to stakeholder management and its results.[3]

Eyes on the Prize: Stakeholder Commitment and Loyalty Building the Business

When we talk about the importance of stakeholders to the business, what should our goal be? Well, for one thing, it shouldn't be limited to "being excellent" or even to "making people happy."The ultimate goal is to earn the commitment of these critical people called stakeholders, and to the degree possible, their loyalty. Institutions have immense strength when constituencies are committed to them. Consider the capital that has been raised by the "dot-com" industry despite a lack of earnings because venture capitalists and other investors remain committed to the concept of continued growth of the Internet and e-commerce. Nordstrom's, deservedly famous for its unmatched service quality, has achieved fierce loyalty among customers, as has John Deere for the quality of its farm and lawn equipment.

Frederick Reichheld has in recent years initiated practical business thinking about stakeholder loyalty in two *Harvard Business Review* articles as well as in his 1996 book, *The Loyalty Effect*. He reminds business leaders of the cumulative cost of customer attrition. Reichheld has recently applied his ideas to employee turnover, but most of his thinking and case studies are on the topic of customer defections.

For example, a 10 percent annual turnover of customers is a low estimate of what U.S. firms average, according to Reichheld. But he reminds us that in just five years, that 10 percent adds up to half of the account base that the business must replace. Profits take an even harder hit, because accounts tend to become more profitable over time. Thus, having even a slight edge over competitors in retaining customers can eventually make a dramatic difference in the relative growth and earnings rates, all else being equal.[4]

To address the issue of customer retention, Reichheld advises first taking account of the financial impact of defections, profiling "the entire lifecycle of profits" that customers are contributing. This equation should include the selling and operating costs for accounts but also profits over time, as well as the impact of referrals to new business that current customers tend to offer. The goal is to increase the retention rate for customers, and counting the costs of defection motivates leadership to make the changes and investment necessary to make that happen.

True Loyalty Means More Than You Might Think. . .

Beyond counting the costs of defections, another tactic for managing business relationships and stakeholder loyalty is to understand what drives loyalty (or the lack thereof). This learning begins when we see that loyalty is more than simply behavior; that is, it is more than just choosing to stay with an organization as an employee, buyer, investor, or supplier. If that were all loyalty meant, then even a corporate spy working for your organization to steal secrets for a competitor would technically be a "loyal" employee as long as he or she were still there! A customer who only grudgingly uses the neighborhood convenience mart and then bad-mouths the high prices to anyone who listens could also be called "loyal."

Experts have concluded that loyalty must contain the right attitude as well as the right action. We use the term *commitment* almost interchangeably with *loyalty* because it embodies more than just "being there." It means also being engaged and supportive and having a "loyal attitude."

Perhaps the best definition of commitment comes from John P. Meyer and Natalie J. Allen, professors at Western Ontario University and authors of *Commitment in the Workplace.* Their research found three types of commitment:

- Emotional (Affective)—having feelings toward an organization; wanting to be associated with it, identifying with its goals or principles, etc.
- Cost-based (Continuance)—weighing the costs of no longer being associated with an organization, and feeling that you *need* to stay
- Obligation-based (Normative)—feeling obligated to remain associated with the organization; feeling a responsibility, or that you *should* stay with an organization because it's the right thing to do[5]

These researchers found that the emotional type of commitment produces the most favorable outcomes—at least related to employee perceptions and behavior—in terms of "retention, attendance, performance, citizenship." In other words, it is better to have earned the commitment of employees in ways that make them want to be there rather than to have them feeling locked-in; they will stay longer with the organization and be more productive.

Other research has indicated that this multidimensional nature of commitment carries over to stakeholders other than employees. The bulk of such research has dealt with customers and the topic of brand or product loyalty. Alan S. Dick and Kunal Basu describe linkage between feelings and behavior in the very way they define customer loyalty, as "repeat purchases prompted by a strong internal disposition."[6] Once again, we see the combination of the action (repeat purchases) with the attitude (strong internal disposition to repeat). These concepts are summarized in Table 3.1.

This equation somewhat follows the maxim, "Win their hearts and minds, and their loyalty will follow." But loyal behavior has other dimensions. A monopoly such as an electric or gas utility can keep customers loyal because the customers have no other options. With the anticipated effects of deregulation, however, utilities will need to think about how to build customer loyalty.

Stakeholders sometimes defect despite having a positive relationship with a company. Loyalty may have been well earned because we met their expectations, but stakeholders still withdraw their support or terminate their relationships with us for other reasons. Employees may have received other offers that were hard to refuse. Customers sometimes simply decide to try other brands or suppliers, just for the sake of switching, or believe in the principle of "not putting all their eggs in one basket."

Loyalty, then, is complex enough to imply that managing stakeholder relationships means more than just doing the right things or even just meeting everyone's expectations. It requires understanding clearly where stakeholders stand and what they think about their relationships with us. We must learn how to assess the current status and inclination of our stakeholders to know how to proceed in our relationships with them.

Stakeholders are simply not all alike in the nature of their loyalty to us. Some customers are more inclined to switch or be loyal than others, and the same could be said about employees, investors, and all other types of constituents of our businesses. To effectively manage those complex relationships, we must find out how stakeholders view their relationship with us and their other options.

TABLE 3.1   Loyalty Equation

Commitment **(Attitude)**	An emotional or psychological attachment to your company, resulting from positive stakeholder interactions
+ Behavior **(Continue with)**	Actions by the stakeholder demonstrating a maintenance or a deepening of the relationship with your company
Loyalty	A stakeholder's endorsement of your company, expressed as an implicit or explicit pledge of continuity in a relationship with you, linked with an attitude of commitment

Classifying the Status of Stakeholder Loyalty

Building on the ideas of Dick and Basu, there is value in evaluating and classifying stakeholders according to different levels of commitment to your firm. Survey research can determine people's position regarding the firm and their loyalty to it. Their answers can be used to position the stakeholders on a spectrum of

- How positive or negative they feel toward the firm and
- How likely or unlikely they are to remain loyal to or continue supporting the firm in the future.

We would normally classify people representing a constituency such as customers or employees in a simple matrix. There are four possible combinations of high and low attitude and behavior in this matrix, so we can segment the stakeholders as being truly loyal, accessible, trapped, or high risk (see Figure 3.1). We will examine the characteristics of and implications for each group.

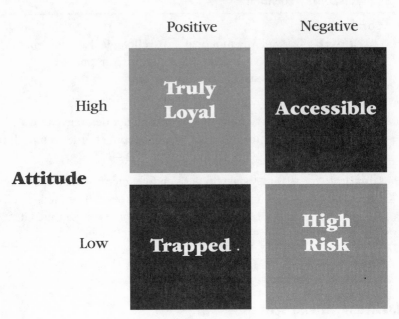

FIGURE 3.1   Stakeholder Loyalty Matrix

Truly Loyal

True loyalty is the ideal—when we have captured not only their feet (loyal behavior) but their hearts and minds as well. Truly loyal stakeholders are positive in both attitude and behaviors. They like their relationship with your company, and they intend to continue or enhance it. As long as these are the constituents the company desires in the first place (strategic stakeholders), then truly loyal stakeholders will be the most productive and profitable ones to have with you over time. The ultimate goal of stakeholder management is to maximize the portion of your strategic stakeholders who are truly loyal and to work at keeping them that way.

Of course, the essence of maintaining loyalty will vary by stakeholder type. Customers are usually satisfied when their expectations have been met or exceeded and when (in their minds) they are getting value for what they are buying. Excellence of product design and quality, a reputable brand, good solutions designed by sales or technical staff, or solving a problem they had been having with another supplier are the elements that make for loyal customers. In addition, convenience and competitive price are minimal requirements.

An employee might be attracted by the compensation and positive work environment you provide and might be loyal because you helped find ways to adjust his or her schedule to spend more time with a new child. Suppliers may stay with you and invest in the relationship for years as long as you pay your bills on time and give them enough time to get your work done right.

Remember that truly loyal stakeholders are not just locked into a relationship with you because they are limited in situation or choices. These are the people who remain associated with you because they want to be, which means they are probably more productive for you. And they are the ones who plan to stay for awhile, which makes them more trustworthy. We all need more of these types of stakeholders.

Accessible

Accessible stakeholders are just that: They like you and are open and accessible to your efforts to earn even greater loyalty from them. They have a positive attitude about the substance of their relationship with you but are holding back from planning to deepen or even definitely continue it. They are keeping their options open.

Stakeholders have many different reasons for not deepening their partnership with you. In many cases, their reasons have little or nothing to do with your company and its relationship with them. A customer may love your products but not want to use you as a sole-source supplier for fear of becoming overly reliant on you or because company policies dictate using multiple suppliers. An employee may be perfectly happy with a job but tend to tire of any one employer over time, or an employee's spouse may be considering a career change and move. A media figure may agree with your company philosophy but be required to maintain an objective distance.

We would anticipate the accessible segment of employee stake-holders to be growing in the age of the new economy because of expanded job opportunities and greater acceptance of frequent job changes. For example, the senior copy editor for *CIO Magazine* testified in a recent article on employee loyalty that he was completely happy in his job—challenged every day, loved his boss, was hopeful about his career, and so forth. "But part of me can't help feeling that I might be missing something by not scanning Monster.com on a daily basis, updating my resume every Sunday night . . . establishing a network of headhunters. I can't shake the feeling that working at one place for four years is a bad thing."[7]

We may not always be able to eliminate the barriers to a longer relationship with accessible stakeholders, whether they are employees, customers, or others. But by learning that they exist and finding out who they are, we put ourselves in a position to remove barriers and try new incentives rather than just being shocked and disappointed when they leave. Remember: These stakeholders are basically pleased with their relationship with us, which makes them open to our communications and our attempts to increase their loyalty. Hopefully, in due time they will move into the truly loyal group.

Trapped

In the bottom half of the matrix are those stakeholders who are not so favorably disposed toward your company and with whom you have not established a positive relationship. The intriguing thing about the trapped segment is that they still exhibit loyalty by their behavior. Even though they don't particularly want to be associated with your organization, they have indicated that they are staying for the time being, hence the term *trapped*. They could be the customers in a regulated environment who have little choice but to do business with your company. They may be employees who are unwilling or unable to find a different job. They may be suppliers under a contract or community leaders who feel they must work with your firm. Again, the reasons will vary but the problem is the same: They would like to end their relationship with you and may do so over time or if their situation changes to allow it.

These stakeholders pose certain threats to your business beyond just the fact that they are inclined to leave. They continue to consume your resources and attention but are not necessarily contributing to your long-term success. Every business has them: the employees who have "quit on the job" (more common and less extreme an example than the corporate spy mentioned earlier, who would also qualify as trapped), the vendor who isn't working all that hard to provide you with the very best products and services, and investors who are only in for what can be gained in the short term.

At the same time, trapped stakeholders (especially employees) represent an opportunity during the time they remain with you. If they are important to your long-term strategy, it is well worth identifying what is keeping them from feeling satisfied. If it turns out to be something you have control over, then countermeasures could be taken to change their opinions and move them into the truly loyal category. If the cost of creating satisfaction exceeds the potential benefit of a healthier relationship with that stakeholder, you may decide that ending the relationship is the best outcome for both parties.

High Risk

Last, and hopefully least prevalent in your business, are the high risk stakeholders. They are not positive about the relationship they have with you, and plan to end it on their own terms. They are the employees conducting job searches from your offices, customers opening your contracts to a competitive bidding process, media stakeholders who don't trust you and are telling people why they don't, and community leaders at cross-purposes with you publicly or who undermine your corporate reputation.

Ideally, you would never want to have any stakeholders in this group. Once they're there, however, and you have the opportunity, you can perform "triage" on the relationship by having a discussion. This dialogue is not for the purpose of turning them suddenly into loyal supporters; often at this stage the only realistic solution is for both parties to go their separate ways. But it is almost always mutually healthy to listen to each other. Instead of simply writing these stakeholders off, communicate with them to clear up any misunderstandings and find any other ways that the company can be of help within reason. This is not only the right thing to do, it can turn an enemy into a neutral party and lessen the chance for bad feelings to be expressed later. Occasionally, this process can even salvage a relationship.

The Four Gates of Engagement

We mentioned previously that business relationships can be harder to maintain as organizations grow in size. This makes it even more important to periodically assess our stakeholders, answering the simple questions, "How do stakeholders feel about us?" and "Do they plan to continue being associated with us?" With answers to those questions, managing the relationships and going forward becomes easier.

Every relationship has a history as well, since they develop and change over time. Remembering that great relationships evolve through different stages of development helps us be proactive in building business relationships the right way. Understanding these stages also promotes the right processes for relating to stakeholders at the stage they are in, from the prospective or brand-new relationship to the longtime associate.

Virtually any successful stakeholder relationship passes through four stages, called the Four Gates of Engagement: Awareness, Knowledge, Admiration, and Action (see Figure 3.2). The gates are generally sequential—each stage of the relationship builds on what was accomplished in the preceding stages. Think of them as locks in a canal. The only way to get to the third lock from the first one is by passing through the second lock. With the gates of engagement, people logically cannot really associate with an organization unless they are aware of it; they can't admire it before gaining some knowledge about it beforehand, and they won't act in a positive way if they don't admire the products, services, and ethics of the enterprise.

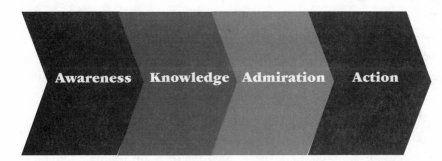

FIGURE 3.2   The Four Gates of Engagement

The main implication of this model is the need to effectively man-age communications with stakeholders of all types. Ultimate engage-ment only comes by building the loyal attitude discussed earlier. Building that attitude requires that companies develop strategies that first create awareness, then deliver information about the company to stakeholders as needed (knowledge). Only by understanding stake-holders' needs well enough can companies encourage admiration over time. By guiding stakeholders' progress through the gates, com-panies can influence and monitor their commitment to the relation-ship.

Let's take a quick tour through each gate of engagement and look at the characteristics that help us discern where stakeholders are in this process. For each gate, we present typical behaviors exhibited by stakeholders.

Gate One: Awareness

Awareness means knowing that something exists. On the surface, this statement would imply that a company should just manage awareness among prospective stakeholders, such as potential customers, employ-ees, suppliers, or supporters in the community. However, we must re-member the "hidden stakeholders," who can and do influence the individuals you already are associated with. For example, business customers should not be your only direct contacts; it is important to recognize that there are many others within the organization beyond your primary contact who have influence on the relationship. How familiar are they with your firm? There are hidden stakeholders in the households of employees and consumers, such as the spouses, who influence the relationship with you. Do these stakeholders really know you?

The first implication of awareness is to make use of technology and maintain an effective database of prospective and hidden stakeholders so that you know something about them and can at least periodically communicate with them. This concept, *database marketing,* is certainly nothing new. What has changed, however, is the greater urgency in a more competitive environment, the new means of database management software and Web technology, and the new paradigm of needing to manage a greater array of stakeholders: potential suppliers or alliance partners conceivably all over the globe (and customers from anywhere as well), regulators, and other third parties. The side benefit of proactively communicating with prospective and hidden stakeholders is that they learn more about you in the process of just creating awareness, and they appreciate that you know who they are. So, effective development of awareness begins to move people beyond just this first stage of engagement. Some indicators of success in creating awareness with prospective stakeholders are depicted in Table 3.2 by constituent type.

Gate Two: Knowledge

The possibilities of sharing knowledge about our organizations today have multiplied with the advent of the Internet and desktop software for packaging and illustrating our products and ideas. The tricky part is that our stakeholders are inundated with information, and we have to figure out how to cut through the "noise" to give them the answers they need or want. Information can be thought of as the sum of all the data that people sift through, like scanning headlines in a newspaper. Knowledge is just the portion that they dig into to learn from, such as when they stop to read an article in detail.

TABLE 3.2   Typical Behaviors of Stakeholders at Gate One: Awareness

Customers	Employees
Know you	Apply for job/sign up for interview
Share at least one contact person	Hit website
You know them	Make queries
	Headhunter shows interest in you

Investors	Suppliers
Know your company/stock exists	Solicit your business
Would take your call/talk to you	

Community	Media
Heard of you	Heard of you
Ask to meet you	

Keep in mind that the two most meaningful types of knowledge that any stakeholder wants to see are those that

- describe a possible solution that could be applied to a problem or need they have and
- interest them by reinforcing your brand/reputation/corporate character.

The first means of providing solutions is obvious in terms of what customers are looking for, but it also applies to prospective employees who need some combination of compensation, career opportunity, and challenges; to community leaders who may be looking for civic contributions, volunteers, or project leadership; and to many other stakeholder groups as well. The key is to find out what the agendas of the different stakeholders and individuals are so that the knowledge content can be targeted. In other words, knowledge is a two-way street: The audience knows you, but you must know something about the audience as well.

TABLE 3.3   Typical Behaviors of Stakeholders at Gate Two: Knowledge

Customers	Employees
See the "fit" for your product/service Want to meet customer support staff/hear more	Know your values, strategy, mission Know the organization's structure and who does what

Investors	Suppliers
Research your company Ask hard questions	Identify your needs Seek feedback on your satisfaction with them

Community	Media
Know what you do/how you do it	Know what you do/how you do it Think about why you matter to them

The second type of knowledge focus has to do with educating your stakeholders about your corporate character. Character is simply the truth about you as a company: the values, culture, and practices of your organization. Reputation is how you're viewed by others. By sharing the truth about your character and by including some lessons learned, as well as successes, you can positively influence the development of your reputation. As stakeholders form an impression of you that is positive and reasonably accurate, you are also moving them through the second gate of engagement. Table 3.3 shows the typical activities in getting each stakeholder group through the knowledge stage of engagement.

Gate Three: Admiration

Once you have established a relationship with stakeholders by sharing the right knowledge about your organization, they are then nearing a point of admiring you, which is the third stage in the relationship. To reach this gate, stakeholders must have reached a point of either trusting that you can help them solve a problem or of simply liking you and wanting to be associated with you. (This is what branding is all about: wanting to be associated with a product or company beyond just the intrinsic value of the product or company itself.) The operative concept is *trust*. You have developed their trust in what your company stands for and/or what it can do for them.

This stage is the point at which a stakeholder has developed what we earlier called a *loyal* or *committed* attitude. Stakeholders want to be associated with you no matter what other barriers exist to having a relationship. Chances are that at this point they would speak highly of your organization if asked. The admiration stage is the ideal time to "close" stakeholders, meaning to seal their trust in you by taking the next step of initiating or deepening the business relationship. That step puts them in the process of moving into the final stage, Action.

Table 3.4 lists the behaviors of different stakeholders that indicate that they have achieved Admiration and might be ready to take the next step of engagement.

Gate Four: Action

The Action gate moves only those stakeholders who are at the top of the loyalty matrix: the truly loyal or accessible groups, whose attitude indicates commitment to (admiration of) your organization. If they are accessible (meaning that they are still not ready to initiate or continue the relationship), it is only due to circumstances outside your control. The truly loyal stakeholders are ready to support your organization more than ever before because you have earned their trust.

By taking steps now to further collaboration with these stakeholders, you can build partnerships that benefit both of you. You will find people willing to recommend you to others and provide word-of-mouth advertising; customers willing to let you deeper into their organization and make additional contacts through their network and

TABLE 3.4   Typical Behaviors of Stakeholders at Gate Three: Admiration

Customers	Employees
Think of you first	Initiate new activities on their own
You have become a trusted supplier	Function without supervision

Investors	Suppliers
Buy stock/make investment	Look for unstated needs/business opportunities
Articulate your company's competitive advantage	

Community	Media
Believe you can/do contribute to the community	Believe you matter to them
	Consider you as a source/expert

distribution channels; and employees willing to take on greater responsibilities as leaders and as role models, with your encouragement and training. The behaviors that demonstrate that stakeholders have reached this stage of engagement are shown in Table 3.5.

....

Case in Point on Stakeholder Commitment: CDW Computer Centers, Inc.

In just 15 years, CDW Computer Centers, Inc. (CDW), considered one of the largest resellers of computing solutions and equipment in the world, has grown from a home-based start-up to well over $2 billion. From the beginning, the values and culture of the company have uniquely blended a passion for technology with a passion for people. The CDW Circle of Service philosophy states: "Everything We Do Revolves Around the Customer." But in addition to fixing on the needs of customers, CDW grants priority attention to its associ-

TABLE 3.5   Typical Behaviors of Stakeholders at Gate Four: Action

Customers	Employees
Refer business, offer testimonials	Refer potential employees
Make you sole-source supplier	Find customers
Engage in collaborative ventures	Innovate
	Act as a role model for peers

Investors	Suppliers
Recommend your stock	Act on your unstated needs
Expand their position	Truly collaborate
Share risk	
Work for your success	

Community	Media
Articulate your contribution	Use you as a source
Tell others	Tell others about you

ates and other stakeholders, as exemplified in CDW's mission statement:

> To be one of the nation's highest volume PC resellers selling name brand products. Provide a fun and challenging work environment, and above-average earnings. Give the customer competitive prices and excellent customer service. Maintain a high net profit by running a lean, highly automated systems-oriented company.[8]

CDW also exemplifies relationship building with its stakeholders through each of the gates of engagement. To move people through the Awareness gate, CDW offers a variety of distribution channels, including direct marketing, retail showrooms and inside salespeople, and an award-winning e-commerce website.

Direct marketing efforts are proactive, including a combination of telemarketing and direct mail catalogs. CDW distributes more than 80 million catalogs annually. They sell only name brand com-

puters as well as name brand accessories, peripherals, and software.

Frequent contacts by marketers and equipping target markets
with catalogs begins to move customers, prospects, and other stakeholders through the Knowledge gate for CDW computer centers.

The website was designed in close cooperation with Microsoft as
part of their Trophy Site program and offers advanced features to
guide any visitor to a better knowledge of the company by answering questions or explaining how to meet product needs.

CDW's commitment to having effective media and investor relations includes a link with direct Web access to the CDW Media
Room and to Investor Relations; the company also offers online access to news releases, articles, and other company information.

First-time corporate callers are immediately assigned an account
manager, which provides them with an additional source for getting questions answered and building their understanding of the
products and services available.

Because knowledge cuts both ways in a good relationship, CDW
has invested in a systematic program that periodically has customers assess CDW and helps CDW in turn assess how to maintain
loyalty with customers. The results are used to manage corporate
accounts more effectively as well as to improve business processes.

The fourth gate, Admiration, hinges on gaining stakeholders'
trust. For CDW that begins with offering customers branded products that themselves are trusted. To build relationships, the company invests in professional development of its customer contact
people. Sales staff members undergo up to four months at CDW
University learning product knowledge as well as solutions-selling
techniques.

In addition to offering them training and the challenging work
environment of a growing technology firm, the company values
employees by fostering balance between their personal and professional needs. In 1999, CDW opened CDW@Play, a 33,000-square-
foot childcare and fitness center, at its Vernon Hills, Illinois,
headquarters. It provides a learning environment for up to 144 children and fitness facilities for weight training, basketball, racquet-
ball, and volleyball.

People in the Chicago area, especially employees of CDW, would be the first to know of the company's support of charitable activities such as Children's Memorial Hospital. Michael Krasny, CEO of CDW Computer Centers, is on record as saying that helping the community will continue to be "not only our duty, but our pleasure."[9] Others have agreed with Krasny that corporate social responsibility is more an obligation to "give back" to communities than about earning the admiration of stakeholders. But over time, such organizations do gain admiration.

Admiration comes even more quickly with awards and recognition by third-party associations or organizations. *BusinessWeek* ranked CDW number six on their annual list of the top 100 information technology companies in the world. CDW has been ranked nineteenth among *Computerworld's* top 100 places to work in IT and was named a finalist for the Better Business Bureau National Torch Award for Marketplace Ethics in the large company category. The award recognizes ethical business interactions with customers and business partners and credits efforts toward corporate citizenship.

These awards also symbolize stakeholders moving through the Action gate of engagement—in this case, third parties recognize the company for its business approaches, not because of its relationship with them but because of its relationship with its owners (investors), customers, employees, community leaders, and others.

As of March 2000, customers had "voted" for CDW by providing net sales of $2.9 billion, a net growth of 52.8 percent and a 24 percent return on equity. Employees helped vote CDW into a top ranking as a place to work, with an all-time high of 2,000 employees. Investors also "voted" as the firm experienced a 181 percent return in shareholder value.

••

Starting at the Beginning

The temptation here is to dive right into the individual stakeholder types and consider the dynamics of deepening relationships with them. However, the next chapter deals with a prerequisite that CDW has accumulated much "equity" in integrity. Business relationships are just like other relationships in that they don't really get off the ground unless people *trust* us. Trust is the essential for dealing with people, and *integrity* is the foundation for trust. So let's discuss integrity next.

Integrity as the Foundation

Integrity: Who Needs It?
(Better Question: Who Doesn't?)

The word *integrity,* and its close cousin, *ethics,* seem to get a lot of play these days in business, which is a healthy sign. It's a very natural topic to be interested in. Think of virtually any type of personal relationship: friend, colleague, family member, and even fleeting acquaintances. Don't we hope to find personal integrity in everyone we know? We seek integrity because it enables us to trust people. And the same holds true for organizations: People want to find integrity in the organizations they work with or buy from.

In fact, we are generally hungry for integrity. A few years ago, a leading thinker on the topic of honesty and integrity stood up to give the commencement address at a university, and began by simply saying he would speak about integrity. The audience erupted into applause. As the speaker, Stephen L. Carter, Yale Law Professor and author of *Integrity* and *The Culture of Disbelief,* recalled, "They had no idea how

I was using the word, or what I was going to say about integrity . . . but they knew they liked the idea of talking about it."[1]

Today, stakeholders don't just want to hear about integrity; they have the leverage to *demand* integrity from organizations. Think of the influence and choices available today for not only customers and employees, but also investors, suppliers, and alliance partners. Internet research for jobs or goods, buying services, consumer guides, chat rooms, online auctions—Have we ever had a greater ability to make informed choices about companies?

Numerous studies in the past several years have concluded that integrity in business practices is a key component of a firm's reputation with its stakeholders, and reputation in turn plays a substantial role in driving commitment to an organization. Research across a variety of industry types shows the impact that integrity and business practices have on reputation and the commitment of various stakeholders:

- Shareholder wealth decreases after a firm acts in a socially irresponsible or illegal manner (reported in *Business and Society*).[2]
- According to the Social Investment Forum (www.socialinvest.org), there has been rapid growth in social investing—to about $1.2 *trillion* in 2000, from just $65 billion in 1985.[3]
- At the end of 1999 there were 47 "Socially Responsible Mutual Funds" tracked by *Business Ethics* magazine.[4]
- If they have negative perceptions about certain businesses, almost eight in ten consumers avoid or refuse to buy from them (Walker's 1994 Corporate Character study).[5]
- Most MBA students will accept 5 to 10 percent lower pay to work for a socially responsible company, reports Ann Svendsen in *The Stakeholder Strategy*.[6]
- Employees are four times as likely to recommend their firm to prospective workers when management acts ethically than when management authorizes improper conduct (KPMG's 2001 Report on Organizational Integrity).[7]

- Employees in ethical organizations are up to six times more likely to be loyal and committed than those in unethical organizations (1999 study of employee retention and business integrity, Walker Information).[8]
- Approximately three in four employees have witnessed an ethical violation, and half of those workers believe the violation could erode public trust if discovered. (KPMG's 2000 Report on Organizational Integrity).[9]

Research consistently shows that investors, customers, and employees are more attracted to and remain committed to organizations with ethical business practices. The downside appears to have even greater impact, with unethical practices undermining commitment or causing stakeholders to avoid certain companies.

Technology has afforded everyone faster networking and better quality of information about companies. In addition (like it or not), there is added pressure from government and NGOs that regulate and monitor industries and companies, including federal and state agencies, socially screened investment funds, "watchdog groups" such as the Sierra Club and the Better Business Bureau, and the local and national media.

Rather than be caught short by a third party or by new regulation and be forced to change through outside pressure, companies are more motivated than ever to initiate programs that evaluate and ensure organizational integrity. We can conclude then that:

1. Integrity is an important component of reputation and of stakeholder commitment.
2. Integrity is a business dynamic that increasingly must be managed, especially in larger organizations.
3. As an increasingly important process to manage, organizational integrity warrants being evaluated and measured periodically.
4. Results of these measures should be used to continue to enhance business integrity.

Before we consider how employees view business practices today and ways in which integrity can be monitored, let's define exactly what we mean by integrity. We will then explore some best practices regarding how integrity is being managed in leading organizations today. We will look more broadly at national business practices based on survey results, then consider a specific measurement application and business case in point.

Integrity Means More Than Just Honesty

Stephen L. Carter, in an *Atlantic Monthly* essay on the topic a few years ago, wrote that integrity means more than just honesty.[10] Honesty, defined as "not lying," is certainly an important virtue, but integrity is more. After all, people frequently seek some threshold of honesty rather than the transparency of real integrity. We see spokespeople for major organizations, not to mention those representing the highest office in the land, regularly choose words that represent honest points of view. But if listeners are being intentionally misled by half-truths, this "honesty" cannot be called integrity.

In Carter's view, there are three steps to determine real integrity:

1. Using principles to discern what is right and wrong.
2. Acting on what has been discerned to be right, even at personal or business cost.
3. Saying openly that you are acting on what you understand to be right versus wrong.

In short, we have integrity when there has been careful consideration of principles or values at stake, when the principle(s) are acted upon even at some personal loss, and when there is openness about the reasoning behind the decision so others can evaluate and have a reason to trust us. Anything less falls short of true integrity.

Core Principles/Values: The Cornerstone

If we agree that true integrity in the workplace requires discernment of right and wrong, then there must be a specific set of values or principles commonly held in the organization. Individuals all have personal values, but the problem is that different people hold to different tenets. And, of course, there can be individuals whose extremely selfish motives and values don't even measure up in the light of the law. The wide diversity of personal values makes it important for organizations to establish common values or principles.

James C. Collins and Jerry I. Porras made this point as a key implication from their research with Stanford University in *Built to Last*. They found that a set of core values embedded in the organizational culture was perhaps the most distinguishing trait among "visionary" companies, that is, ones "widely admired by their peers and having a long (50+ year) track record of making a significant impact on the world around them."[11] Their list of 18 companies meeting the visionary criteria included 3M, American Express, Boeing, Hewlett-Packard, Johnson & Johnson, Nordstrom, and Walt Disney.

These long-term all-stars were distinguishable even from other strong and enduring firms by having a "core ideology," meaning a small set of principles or values and a sense of purpose beyond just that of making money. The core values served as guidelines and as an inspiration for the employees. Through the years and a succession of leaders, it was always clear that the company's tenets were never to be compromised. And it was also crucial that the values were authentic, meaning they flowed naturally from the history of the culture and what the business was really about, rather than just being created and then imposed from the top.

Consider the example of Merck & Company offered by Collins and Porras. As early as 1935, decades before it became popular to develop organizational value statements, George Merck II was articulating specific ideals as being commonly held within the institution. He described a value that the company had long tried to live up to: "Medicine is for the patient . . . for the people . . . not for the profits." In the culture at Merck, not only the medical professionals but also business leaders, scientists, and clerks believed in that principle.

In a reported case of how the institution acted in accordance with its ideals, the company decided to give away the drug Metazoan to cure river blindness, a horrific parasitic condition in which the parasites ultimately destroy the eyes in a painful and permanent blindness. At first there had appeared to be a market, in a sense, for more than a million people in need of the product. Yet these customers were unable in the foreseeable future to afford a new drug. Despite projections of minimal to no return on investment, the company proceeded in developing the drug, hoping that there would be financing from third parties or agencies. When these options fell through, Merck decided simply to give the drug away at its own expense, because "medicine is for the patient."

In case it needs to be said, Merck & Company, along with the other companies in the Stanford study, has been extremely profitable over a long period of time despite making principle-based (versus just profit-based) decisions. In fact, the performance of the values-driven companies in stock returns over more than 60 years was more than 15 times that of the general stock market.

The researchers concluded that adhering to an ideology and exhibiting integrity energizes not only people in the organization but those who work with it. A combination of committed customers, employees, investors, and partners indisputably contributes to successful performance over long periods of time.

What other core values do companies have, and are certain values common across firms? A 1999 paper on corporate values related how Rose Ann Stevenson, an HR manager at Boeing, studied the values of 77 different companies.[12] Most commonly mentioned were integrity, involvement, achievement, quality, creativity/innovation, and respect. Because there were so many different interpretations of what these common values meant, her study indicates how important it is for leaders to translate a value into specific actions that clarify the meaning to all associates.

Core values are critical to good business practices because employees can learn to apply them to many different situations. Policies and laws can never cover all situations, and even if they could, there would be too many for anyone to remember. As we shall see, values or principles are not the only resource needed to manage integrity. But like the cornerstone in the foundation, values and principles serve to anchor the rest.

Ethics: Principles in Action

Ethics is defined as behaving in accordance with the values or standards that are in place. This definition distinguishes ethics from *compliance,* which means adhering to rules, laws, and regulations. Thus, when a Merck decides to act on its principles, it is behaving ethically.

Achieving good business ethics and compliance is not as simple as establishing the core values of the institution or even posting the laws and then assuming that employees adhere to them. In fact, as described later in this chapter, many corporations have already invested in tools for managing integrity, including codes of conduct or ethics, ethics offices, and company-wide training in business ethics. Organizational ethics or compliance is in fact becoming another business process not unlike quality management, with its own professional associations, consultants, and national awards.

However, even with a solid ethics program in place, the innate challenge of managing ethics in a large organization still comes down to decision making at the individual level. As Michael Gropp, Chief Compliance Officer of Guidant Corporation, states, "Compliance (or the same might be said for ethics) is the net result of thousands of decisions made on a day-to-day basis by individuals at all levels in the organization."[13] In Guidant's case, as in an increasing number of institutions, these thousands of decisions are being made all over the globe every day in a variety of geographic and business cultures.

Factors in Ethical Decision Making

Managing business ethics must account then for individual decision making. But what drives the individual decision-making process? From the work of experts in the field, we conclude that individual decisions are affected by the situation or the intensity of the ethical situation; the personal values of the individual involved; and organizational factors, such as leadership examples, how others in the company behave, and how and why people are promoted.

This complexity in business decision making is illustrated in Figure 4.1, from *Integrity Management*. It implies how important it is to have commonly held values to help guide decisions made by different people in various situations.[14]

Leaders of organizations and teams need to understand this model because they have an opportunity to influence nearly all facets of ethical decision making. A 1997 study, co-sponsored by the Ethics Officer Association and the Society of Financial Services Professionals, showed that six in ten U.S. workers feel they are under a substantial amount of pressure to perform at work, and 56 percent feel some pressure to act unethically or illegally on the job.[15] The highest reported unethical actions included cutting corners on quality control, covering up incidents, abusing or lying about sick days, and lying to or deceiving customers.

We can't forget that there are factors in the workplace that actually work against good ethical decisions. If we as leaders simply assume there will be ethical behavior, then we fail to admit there are enough real workplace pressures and conflicts of interest to counter the best programs and intentions. Leaders need to be the first to exemplify that the organization will meet its goals by playing within the boundaries of values, ethics, and laws. In addition to leading by example, good policies and training programs that teach employees how to make the right decisions are effective in countering workplace pressures.

These individual factors cannot be ignored, because organizations rely on strong individuals and must allow them autonomy. Individuals

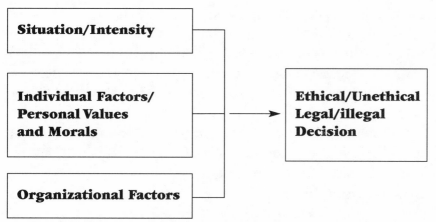

FIGURE 4.1   Factors Underlying Ethical Decisions.
   Source: Debbie Leclair, O. C. Ferrell, and John Fraederich, *integrity Management*
(Tampa: University of Tampa Press, 1998), p. 33.

do bring their personal values (or lack thereof) into the workplace. Management needs to face up to the challenge of dealing with high-performing associates at all levels who break the rules or compromise values along the way. What management does or doesn't do with such people sends a clear message to associates.

Porras and Collins relate that their "visionary" companies tend to be quite demanding about people adhering to the culture and core values. "Because the visionary companies have such clarity about who they are, what they're all about, and what they're trying to achieve, they tend to not have much room for people unwilling or unsuited to their demanding standards."[16] Great care is taken in screening applicants and in training and orienting them to the culture. Most of these companies rely heavily on promotion from within. There is great diversity in these companies, some receiving accolades for the opportunities they provide minorities and women. They clearly want all kinds of people on their team—*as long as they believe in what the company stands for.*

If an employee does not completely deviate from the culture but instead is more borderline in adapting to the standards, there is reason to hope that he or she can make the changes needed. Many workers can rise to new standards of ethics. In a survey by the Ethics Resource Center, nearly half of the 4,000 respondents believed that their own business ethics had been enhanced over the course of their careers, and 13 percent believed that their business ethics had even improved their personal ethics.[17]

This last point is an indication of the impact that organizational culture can have on individual decision making, changing not only behavior through its influence, but potentially even personal values. Remember that the values in the visionary companies served not only to guide but actually to inspire the associates.

On the other hand, many of us can relate to how improper behavior or misconduct in a work team or culture can ultimately become contagious. Whether it be not telling the truth on reports or accepting improper gifts from suppliers, misconduct seems to come easier when "everyone does it" than when such an act is considered taboo in the culture.

Dealing with the Complexity of Ethical Issues

Managing integrity and ethics would be simpler if the issues were always clear-cut. But because they are not, there is a growing number of training programs and consultants in this profession. Michael Rion, author, corporate ethics manager, and now consultant, has spent a career sorting through the complexity of issues faced by managers and instructing leaders on ethical decision making. He explains that one category of ethical issue is when the ethical obligation or "right thing to do" seems clear, but the choices involved are tough ones. Consider, for example, if a colleague were being treated unfairly by a team leader or executive. Even when an injustice seems clear, do we always speak up in support of the colleague at the risk of defying the one who is in authority? The fact is that the right thing to do simply does not always seem prudent (which doesn't make it any less right). Rion says that although there are always a few selfish individuals who ignore ethical standards, "Right action is sometimes easier to talk about than to do, even for persons with high moral standards."[18] At the same time, there are many cases in which people know the right thing to do but aren't sure quite how to go about doing it. In these situations, values, training, and decision-making tools come in handy to point people in the right direction.

Another situation occurs when the ethical answer to a problem is simply unclear. For example, when there is no policy, is it wrong to handle two customers differently in terms of servicing or pricing? How do we know the point at which it is time to terminate an employee versus giving that person another chance? Rion says that *fairness* seems to lurk as the element behind most of these ethical dilemmas where the right answer is not clear.

A third type of ethical dilemma arises when there clearly is more than one right answer, or "competing claims." The classic case here is the unwritten principle of commercial enterprises to remain financially solvent no matter what. In a down period financially, this mindset leads to cost-cutting measures that affect people's lives—some lose their jobs and others must pick up the slack in their own workloads. What is the ethical way to proceed?

Another common case of competing claims would be a remote, but potentially dangerous, safety or environmental problem, where the fix for the problem would mean an enormous financial investment, one that is not legally required. How does one sort through the ethics when clearly one important principle will be followed while another is violated no matter what decision is made?

Rion offers a framework for working through dilemmas faced in any of these categories in *The Responsible Manager.* He teaches managers to carefully consider six questions when proceeding to resolution:

1. Why is this issue bothering me?
2. Who else matters or will be affected by the decision?
3. Is it my problem?
4. What is the ethical concern—legal obligation, fairness, honesty, doing good?

5. What do others think?
6. Am I being true to myself/could I share my decision with my family and closest friends? [19]

By using this framework, managers narrow their ethical decision making to more manageable proportions when facing a difficult decision. Rion agrees with other experts that such a framework works best within the broader context of a values-driven culture, with top management support and other means of supporting integrity, such as ethics codes/policies, dedicated staff, helplines, and professional training. In addition, there are numerous supporting professional associations, nonprofit resource groups, government regulations, and specialty consultants in the field. Each of these resource options is briefly described below.

Types of Integrity Management Resources

Coming out of its experience setting guidelines for defense contractors, the United States Sentencing Commission received approval in 1991 for its Federal Sentencing Guidelines (FSGs). These guidelines provided accountability for business practices and made it clear that business organizations and their leaders would be held responsible for criminal acts of employees. Significantly, the FSGs offered major incentives for companies to establish specific internal resources that the government felt would help prevent misconduct and promote good corporate citizenship. The incentives were in the form of reduced fines for companies complying with the guidelines and increased fines for those that had not been in compliance at the time a criminal act occurred.

The Federal Sentencing Guidelines almost certainly accelerated the installation of ethics resources in companies. By the late 1990s, the vast majority of companies had made headway in introducing integrity management programs and infrastructure in accordance with FSGs. The most prevalent types of resources are described below.

Code of Ethics

Our studies have shown that, along with values, a code of ethics or code of conduct is the most prevalent ethics resource used in U.S. companies.[20] These standards of conduct for the organization are longer and more detailed by design than the core values. Experts tend to agree that the code of ethics or conduct and the values should be closely aligned; in essence, the code spells out ways in which the values are to be upheld. The code should essentially explain how the company shall (and shall not) conduct its day-to-day business.

Most companies creating or updating their codes today try to focus on the most common issues and problems, to keep the content concise. Some firms require all managers or all associates to testify with their signature that they have read and understood the current document.

Ethics Officers

Many large organizations today have charged a senior manager with the overall responsibility for the ethics or compliance program. This was a specific recommendation in the FSGs, but it also emphasizes the investment by companies to make their programs more than just "window dressing," having a code but making little change in the culture. The ethics/compliance officer frequently reports to the board as well as to top management and is responsible for activities such as informing others of the FSGs and all other regulations affecting the business and coordinating training or other means of enhancing compliance and ethical practices in the culture. The ethics/compliance officer also has the responsibility for receiving reports of misconduct; investigating further as needed; and with the help of a committee, judging each case. The acceptance of ethics/compliance officers within corporations is evident from the growth of professional support groups: The Ethics Officers Association has grown from its start in 1994 to over 600 members in 2000, and the Health Care Compliance Association has experienced explosive growth in the late 1990s as well.

Integrity Communications, Training, and Development

The first goal of integrity training is to follow the recommendation of the FSGs to communicate the code of conduct, regulations, and other ethical procedures in a way that can be easily referenced and followed by employees. Beyond just distributing and reviewing documents, an increasing number of firms are conducting professional or even video training sessions. Many of these present scenarios are true-to-life ethical dilemmas that employees face. As mentioned previously, others are using decision-making models that provide associates with a tool for applying integrity to a variety of situations.

The case for training and communications was actually made previously when we discussed core values versus individual ones: We cannot leave to chance that every individual will interpret corporate values or a code of conduct in the same way. In addition, people need to be reminded that the business wants them to make ethical decisions. Business people generally don't need reminders to make shrewd business decisions, but it makes a difference to remind people that certain principles and laws take precedence over that which benefits the business or individual. So, we communicate and train in ways that present the best way for the business to be run in the face of ethical dilemmas.

In *Ethics Matters,* Dawn-Marie Driscoll and Michael Hoffman describe the scope and flexibility of ethics communications in the Olin Corporation, a $1.4-billion manufacturer of copper alloy and other metals and chemicals. With 6,500 employees, and "integrity" heading up the short list of Olin's corporate values, Robert Gebring, Vice President of Auditing, Business Ethics, and Integrity, summed up the importance of ethics communications: "You (as a manufacturing firm) have to keep repeating and varying the safety message, to keep people focused. Ethics and values are no different."[21]

This company reinforces its most important ethical issues and corporate values by posting signs on bulletin boards, putting out promotional items, distributing issue-specific brochures, and, increasingly, updating information on its website. The communications are augmented by classroom training on ethics and values as well, but Gebring firmly believes that formal training must be reinforced with effective and frequent communications. This point about continual reinforcement was echoed by Victoria Wesseler, President of Ethics and Compliance Strategies of Indianapolis. She said that "the biggest mistake made by any firm training its employees is when it focuses too much on the initial effort, and forgets that training must be an ongoing activity—consistency of effort over time is the key."[22]

An effective communications and training approach to integrity management in any organization helps counter at least three enemies of ethical work practices:

1. Business goals and related work pressures: Learning the importance of specific principles and policies, employees are given a rationale for balancing business performance with ethical practices.

2. Ignorance and apathy: Anyone spending time in a large organization (especially any Dilbert fan) has seen programs that are like a "rocket launch"—exciting when they start, but soon the precepts of the program fade out of sight, out of mind. Repeated communications and training also bring the values and code of conduct to life, rather than leaving them dwelling in a handbook, little noticed.

3. The "ethical rogue" in the organization: Many organizations have tolerated to varying degrees the rule bender (or rule breaker) who is otherwise a high performer. Although a degree of tolerance and diversity of style is always good, such individuals can create serious problems if the institution's policies regarding laws and essential principles are not made visible and enforced. When values are communicated and enforced, the "rogues" are at least made to feel isolated.

Ultimately, they will adjust their behavior, leave, or be terminated before all other efforts to manage integrity are undermined, or worse, a criminal act is committed.

Auditing and Monitoring

Not all companies think about monitoring or auditing, especially when they are scrambling to implement a new process or program. On the other hand, the question is irrefutable: How do we know our ethics program and business practices are up to our values and standards unless we measure them?

Most ethics or compliance offices establish a "helpline" or other open form of interaction so they can stay on top of the types of questions being asked and the dilemmas that employees need advice about. Analyzing this activity offers some measure of employee behavior and of program effectiveness. These helplines or "hotlines" also offer employees a special outlet for reporting unethical or criminal conduct. This fulfills one of the recommendations of the FSGs.

Many companies are beginning to conduct more formal audits of employee behavior in relation to the corporate values and code of conduct. An inside or outside auditor works with a comprehensive checklist that carefully assesses business practices across various departments and teams. Based on the findings, refinements are made to the organizational structure and the integrity management program.

Organizational surveys are a relatively untapped but effective means of monitoring integrity as well. Because employees are "where the action is" regarding business practices, they are a logical source of feedback regarding how the behavior of the organization matches up to its stated values and standards. Surveys similar to those used inside an organization can offer a useful perspective on national and industry tendencies regarding integrity in the workplace.

So How Are We Doing (Ethically)?

National studies give us an indication of how well integrity is being managed in organizations today, and the "report card" says we have at best a mixed bag—some positives, but much room to improve as well. In 1999 Walker Information teamed with Hudson Institute, the think tank known internationally for its work assessing national and community workforce needs, to study the perceptions of U.S. employees in organizations having at least 50 workers. Key findings from the questions on workplace ethics are discussed below.[23]

Views Are Mixed on Integrity in the Workplace

- Less than half (47 percent) believe that their senior leaders are people of high integrity.
- A slight majority feel that integrity has been well-communicated internally (56 percent).
- A similar number say there is little pressure to cut corners on ethical/compliance issues (55 percent).
- A majority (59 percent) say their organization is highly ethical, 25 percent are neutral or not sure, and 16 percent do not believe their workplace is highly ethical.

Worker Reluctance to Report Ethical Violations

- Only one-third (34 percent) feel comfortable reporting misconduct, due in part to just 42 percent feeling that ethical or compliance problems are dealt with fairly or completely.
- The majority of employees who saw or knew about a violation have *not* reported it (60 percent).
- Primary reasons given for not reporting actual observed misconduct:

1. Did not feel the organization would respond
2. Lack of anonymous/confidential means of reporting
3. Fear of retaliation from management

Types of Integrity Violations Occurring

- Nearly one-third of all employees (30 percent) have top-of-mind recall of ethical violations in their organizations in the past two years. (*Note:* The incidence of those seeing violations goes up when respondents are asked about specific violations. KPMG's 2000 survey report found 75 percent recalling a problem when asked about 22 specific potential violations.)[24]
- The top seven violations are
  1. Unfair treatment of employees
  2. Lying on reports or falsifying records
  3. Lying to supervisors
  4. Stealing/theft from employer
  5. Conflicts of interest
  6. Sexual harassment
  7. Abusing drugs/alcohol

Some Industry Sectors Struggle with Integrity Issues More than Others

Following are integrity rankings from the highest-rated to the lowest-rated, based on an employee perception index of

1. Financial Services
2. Technology
3. Insurance
4. Health Services
5. Retail

6. Communications
7. Manufacturing
8. Government
9. Transportation

Integrity at Work Relates to Employee Commitment and Loyalty

- Employees were more *truly loyal* (both committed to the organization and planning to stay) when they believed their workplace had ethical practices.
- In contrast, the employees with negative views of workplace integrity were more likely to be *trapped* (low commitment, yet staying) or *at risk* (low commitment and low intention of staying)
- More than half (55 percent) of those rating their organization as highly ethical are *also truly loyal;* this compares with just 24 percent of those neutral about the ethics at work and just 9 percent of those who do not believe their organization is ethical.

The most disturbing result of this study to the researchers was that not even half of the people working today believe the leaders of their organizations have integrity. We know from additional statistical analysis that this impression of top management drives the overall image that employees have of the integrity of where they work. It also begs the question, why? Why aren't organizational leaders more admired for their integrity?

Looking to the survey for clues, we noticed that the industry generally viewed as highest for integrity by its workers and managers, Financial Services, also had dramatically higher ratings of leadership integrity than any other industry. Financial Services in this case represents banking, credit card, or securities organizations.

Financial institutions, to which we all regularly turn over our assets (and debt accounting) must abide by hard-and-fast rules for handling other people's money. We would argue that no other industry has more effectively sold its trustworthiness to stakeholders than this one. Apparently, in the minds of the employees, their leaders are exemplifying the high standards, either self-imposed or regulated, that are a way of business in this category. So the questions to managers in every industry should be: Are you exemplifying the highest standards for your industry? Are you leading in a fashion that even begins to earn the level of trust that stakeholders have in their financial institutions?

We also notice that, to employees, business ethics begins at home, with the degree of fairness with which the company deals with its own associates. Note that the top "violation" cited in the study was "employees being treated unfairly." Financial institutions were dramatically lower than the norm for this complaint. In the January 2000 *Fortune* "100 Best Companies to Work For," five of the top ten best employers were financial institutions: Synovus Financial, Edward Jones, Charles Schwab, Goldman Sachs, and MBNA.[25] The message to leaders is that it will be hard to communicate integrity unless the associates are seeing fairness in their own relationships with the company, in terms of pay/benefits/career opportunities, keeping promises, equality of opportunities and rewards, life/work balance policies, and so forth.

Another message to leaders from the national study is to maintain a more "open society" at work, encouraging the reporting of integrity issues. Some problems will have to be rooted out, but they won't come to light unless people believe that the leadership values integrity highly enough to want them reported and dealt with. Otherwise, we may only get to see problems after they are reported outside our organizations.

A final point regarding the study is the clear message about employees being more committed and loyal when there is integrity in the workplace. It is not too hard to begin making a business case for good ethics when we see that ethical companies can count over half of their workers as committed and loyal, compared to only 9 percent for the unethical organizations.

Using a Business Integrity Survey

An increasing number of organizations today are using survey questions to help maintain a check on perceptions and issues regarding integrity of practices as well as the program within their organizations. The Walker/Hudson Institute question set or questions like those could be tracked in your own organization, either as a standalone survey or as a module within a broader employee survey. These questions also have become a standard portion of a comprehensive organizational survey of issues that drive employee commitment.

A similar approach to assessing integrity and monitoring perceptions is being deployed as part of the integrity management client engagements by many leading consulting firms, notably KPMG's Integrity Management Services practice.

As with any employee survey, identities of respondents are kept confidential and the questionnaires are sent to a third party for processing. Although surveys measure perceptions more than actual behavior, the findings do assess the needs of different parts of the organization regarding ethics communications and training. Employee observations about practices also offer a leading indicator of actual behavior, particularly when respondents report unethical tendencies/pressures or ethical/legal problems that previously have gone unreported.

•••

Case in Point: Niagara Mohawk— Monitoring Values and Integrity with Surveys

Niagara Mohawk Holdings, Inc., is headquartered in Syracuse, New York. This investor-owned utility, which serves more than 1.5 million electric and 540,000 gas customers in upstate New York, is listed among the 30 largest investor-owned utilities in the United States and is in the Fortune 500.

The utility industry is in the process of being deregulated along the lines that telecommunications was in the 1980s, so cultural

changes in utilities are advancing today even faster than in most industries. With those changes at Niagara Mohawk have come the
need to address ethical issues, such as keeping the regulated business separate from unregulated subsidiaries, meeting rising customer expectations of service, and improving employees'
understanding of the company's expectations.

Under the leadership of Niagara Mohawk's Chairman and CEO,
William E. Davis, the company decided in 1997 to reemphasize and
bolster its ethics program. This included a thorough review of the
program, with a focus on the following issues:

- Strengthening the organizational structure supporting ethics
- Reinforcing a culture of integrity
- Revamping the code of conduct
- Revitalizing the ethics training
- Using the company's five core values to drive the ethics
  initiative[26]

The immediate organizational changes started with the appoint-
ment of a Vice President of Ethics who reports directly to the CEO.
An ethics oversight committee of senior officers, chaired by the CEO,
was created to keep senior management engaged in ethics issues and
policy making. Steps were taken to involve line management more in
ethics by directing them to handle disciplinary issues in coordination
with the ethics officer; by including ethics management criteria in
their performance evaluations; and by expecting them to discuss ethical issues regularly with their teams.

As part of the ethics revitalization, Dr. W. Michael Hoffman, Executive Director of the Center for Business Ethics at Bentley College,
was engaged to assess Niagara Mohawk's ethics program and provide improvement ideas. During 1999, the company involved virtually every employee in half-day ethics training program sessions
that entailed case studies, the code of conduct, ethical dilemmas,
and reminders of the resources available through the ethics office.

To help monitor its progress, Niagara Mohawk conducted a baseline employee ethics survey. The main objectives were to not only
assess training needs, but gauge employees orientation to the com-

pany's core values. After comparing the 1999 baseline survey a follow-up survey a year later, employee ratings of ethical issues were
notably higher on virtually every survey item.

....

Have You Checked the Foundation?

We should consider it at least worth posing this question to executive staff: Are we perceived as trustworthy? What are the cues that
people—our employees, our customers, our suppliers or other partners—take about our integrity as a company?

In the United States, one common denominator for ethics program
assessment is to assure that the organizations meet the best practices
described by the FSGs for organizations. Those guidelines can be
summed up in seven steps (adapted from Driscoll and Hoffman):

1. Establish compliance standards and procedures (Code of
   Conduct)
2. Assign high-level individuals to oversee compliance
   (Corporate Ethics and Compliance Officer/VP)
3. Exercise due care in delegating discretionary authority
4. Communicate and train
5. Monitor, audit, and provide safe reporting systems
6. Enforce appropriate discipline with consistency
7. Respond to offenses and prevent recurrences[27]

The previously mentioned Ethics Officer Association (EOA), a non-
consulting professional association for those directly managing integrity programs in their firms, has fostered a great deal of
self-assessment by member firms, who are encouraged to share resources and learning from their efforts to follow the FSGs and other
best practices. At their website, www.eoa.org, the EOA regularly posts
links to the program elements from member firms in various industries.

The elements include electronic versions of ethics office resources, codes of conduct, brochures on industry-specific regulations, self-training modules, ethics-related articles, and speeches. The EOA also sponsors national conferences and other forums for sharing best practices.

Beyond self-assessment, the EOA also recognizes the important contributions made by consultants in the field, which extend not only to helping firms establish best practice programs and training employees but also to assisting them in meeting FSG step five: to monitor, audit and provide safe reporting systems. Arguably, a third party brings objectivity to such activities, whether by offering an 800-number service for reporting violations or by performing audits or assessments to evaluate program effectiveness.

The EOA recently compiled a resource guide for compliance program assessment based on surveying the methods deployed by leading consultants to this growing profession, including KPMG, Pricewaterhouse Coopers, and 12 other smaller agencies based in the United States and Canada. The services related to monitoring ethics invariably entail some form of interview or questionnaire administered to employees at all levels. The objective is to measure the awareness and acceptance of the corporate values and code of conduct and to determine the degree to which decision making at all levels is in line with those guidelines.

If an organizational assessment or more obvious evidence of problems indicates that trust in your firm has been diminished, it can be restored. But remember that addressing these issues and renewing that trust provides a foundation for (and must precede) other opportunities to build relationships and loyalties with stakeholders. Restore trust, then figure out how to maintain it as well. One of the first places to renew those efforts is to target the loyalty among an important stakeholder group, your customers. Customer loyalty is discussed as a management issue in the next chapter.

The Power of Customers

I f you want to have an interesting philosophical discussion about your business sometime, ask your colleagues, "Which stakeholder is more important to us, our customers or our employees?" Based on the results of a recent study, you might have an argument on your hands!

The Walker Information Global Network in early 1999 surveyed 1,027 executives from large corporations throughout the world to evaluate understanding and practices regarding stakeholder measurement and management. The study found that customers and employees are universally recognized as stakeholders (93 percent of all executives cite each type). Customers were given the slight edge in importance overall, but in at least three countries—the United States, Canada, and South Africa—employees are rated nearly as important to decision making as customers (employees were rated as important by more than 90 percent of the executives, whereas customers were rated as important by more than 95 percent).[1] We aren't going to jump in the middle of that argument, except to say this: Customers

91

and employees warrant being recognized as your most important stakeholders because without either one, you cannot have a viable business. Their commitment is critical, and one of the keys to gaining their trust is first to understand and then to address their needs. We discuss the management of customer relationships in this chapter and focus on employee relationships in Chapter 6.

Customer Focus—or Else

Emphasizing that customers are critical to one's business is, of course, not exactly a new phenomenon. Customer focus was given tremendous emphasis toward the end of the twentieth century as organizations adopted "searches for excellence" and various forms of Total Quality Management (TQM). Business movements like these only come about to fill a void and to embody principles that have somehow been left out in the course of human business events. The excellence and TQM movements created an important foundation for where we are today.

The fact is that by the 1970s, many U.S. businesses were simply not consistently meeting customers' wants and needs well enough to differentiate themselves from global competition. The U.S. post-war economy of the 1950s and early 1960s experienced economic prosperity against limited competition, and businesses concentrated on building production capacity and organizational structures.

The Xerox Corporation's experience during this period illustrates how a renewed customer focus helped counter getting caught behind global competition in offering customers value. For a decade and a half after its inception, Xerox was a classic "category-maker"— perceived to be the best in a category where even the competitive products were called "Xerox machines" and making a copy was "Xeroxing."

By the mid-1970s, however, the firm was being challenged by competitive products, especially from Japan, that were not only more reliable and functional but had lower costs as well. This value challenge eroded Xerox's world market share as they found their products in some categories to be not even second-best.

In 1984, an aggressive quality improvement program was launched. In retrospect it could have been termed "value improvement," because a dramatic change in manufacturing processes, employee and supplier training, union relationship agreements, and supply choice management led to a dramatic reduction of per-unit cost as well as improvements in the reliability and functional quality of the copier products.

Of great assistance at this time was input from Fuji Xerox, a joint alliance Xerox had in Asia with Fuji Film. Fuji Xerox had independently developed products and processes to compete in Japan and had become a critical benchmarking partner for Xerox in setting goals for its new mission.

The engine for the changes at Xerox was threefold:

1. Customer feedback
2. Teamwork
3. Measurement of improvement

It included an extensive customer service measurement system that tracked feedback in terms of the preferences and loyalty of approximately 200,000 Xerox equipment owners. Teamwork came from the 7,000 or so teams of workers for process improvement, the joint meetings with almost 500 suppliers for improving their processes and contributions, and the unions to establish joint commitment to the new organizational design. New measurements of improvement became a benchmarking system that tracked 240 key areas of product, service, and business performance.

The outcomes of this effort within five years included the following:[2]

- A 78 percent decrease in product defects
- Increased product reliability, indicated by a 40 percent decrease in unscheduled maintenance

- Improved copy quality
- A 27 percent drop (nearly two hours) in service response time
- The ability to offer an industry-first three-year warranty

The quest for success, of course, is never ending. But one of the single outcomes of Xerox refocusing the entire firm on increasing value for customers was the development of its renowned 10-series, a new family of mid-volume copiers that debuted in the mid-1980s. On the strength of the record-breaking success of that series and improvement in other lines as well, the company won back much of its market share and restored its bottom line and its morale at the same time.[3]

Even on a micro level, when a business is growing quickly, the natural tendency is to worry less about managing relationships and customer loyalty than just about managing operational capacity, hiring and training, and other aspects of managing growth. A recession in the 1970s and global competition in the 1980s were wake-up calls for U.S. industry to recognize that it had taken its eyes off providing customers with what they ultimately wanted.

Evolving Metrics for Customer Relationship Management

There has been somewhat of an evolution in the key metric or goal to use with customers, or at least in what to call it. The catch phrase throughout the 1980s was "customer satisfaction"; in the 1990s businesses realized that customers actually were seeking more than just satisfaction. They were seeking value for the money paid, which clearly entailed a combination of product, service, and in many cases, brand or image.

By the end of the 1990s, however, it had become clear that even value was not the final answer with regard to managing customer relationships. The customer emphasis in the early twenty-first century is *loyalty*. We have defined stakeholder loyalty as both having a committed attitude and planning to remain associated with your business for some period of time. When it comes to customers, loyalty is the reward for truly understanding customer needs and acting on that knowledge. Remember that in today's world, customers in the markets you want to serve strategically may hear of a competitive offering or a new technology and decide that they want an entirely different approach than the product or service you have been providing.

What do customers want and expect when they buy (or repurchase)? They want a useful service or product, a solution to a problem, some level of emotional connection with the product or the company brand, or some mix of both a solution and the brand identity.

When a customer is seeking a business solution with the purchase of products and services from a supplier, then that product or service must have features that make it competitive, such as a lower price, easier or more functional use, or better customer service. Marketers also work hard and spend sizable resources to establish recognized, attractive brands, because the emotional connection to the brand can be a tiebreaker for customers choosing between competing products. In some cases, brand loyalty may be the main reason for buying, such as with loyal buyers of Coca-Cola. Think also of those who order their liquor by the brand in restaurants or who are proud to be driving their second or third Lexus or Saturn.

Business must "get inside the minds" of their customers and understand the psychology of purchasing in the markets they serve. Do you know exactly why your customers buy your products or services or why they choose to repurchase or switch to another brand? With the goal being to build longer relationships to retain customers, it helps to explore the ways to do this at each stage of the relationship cycle, or, to employ the concept introduced in Chapter 3 once again, consider how your customers best proceed through the gates of loyalty.

Gate One: Customer Awareness

What are the best ways for your customers to become aware of your firm and its offerings?

- Do you know how customers first become aware of you?
- How are those patterns of customer awareness evolving? (Are you tracking "cold" queries on your website and from various links to the sites of other organizations?)
- Are you getting the visibility you want when customers learn of you through channel or alliance partners?

Gate Two: Customer Knowledge

- What do you want customers to know about your products and services?
- What are the best means of conveying that knowledge, based on experiences with your most strategic accounts and their feedback?
- How can you help customers more effectively utilize your products and services (even to the point of growing the whole product category—helping competitors as well)?

Gate Three: Customer Admiration (of Your Firm)

- Do you know the favorable elements of your product/service offerings that set you apart from competitors?
- Are these same elements touted in your marketing communications with customers?
- Are your own or your channel partners' systems equipped to handle any increasing desire among customers for more individual attention (customized, "one-to-one" marketing)?
- Do you know what your corporate reputation is and how customers weigh their image of your firm into their mix of buying criteria? Do you know how your image is conveyed or reinforced by channel partners?

Gate Four: Customer Actions

- Which types of business-to-customer or business-to-business accounts are the most profitable/best fit for your long-term strategy?
- Which customer actions should you set measures on (e.g., your "customer-buy" ratio at customer point-of-decision, repurchase rate, perceived loyalty and commitment, share of wallet)?
- Do you know the key elements that drive loyalty among the most profitable segments? If you are business-to-business, what drives loyalty with the most influential members of the buying "committee?"

Of course, the mix of elements on which to focus marketing, sales, and account management resources varies for different customer segments. For example, the largest accounts, national/multinational accounts or consumer "heavy-users" usually negotiate harder on price and demand more service than does the average buyer. Another sobering reality is that we can have the right mix of services, product quality, price, and corporate image in place, and still lose customer loyalty if we fail to understand the evolving needs of customers. Customer loyalty is a tough thing to manage right now, which, of course, makes it even more critical.

The State of Customer Loyalty

A unique database of customer loyalty feedback from various companies and industries has been sorted and analyzed by Walker Information according to the loyalty segments described in Chapter 3. It provides evidence that enterprises are challenged in their management of customer loyalty. This database is made up of thousands of customers across 84 different customer studies in financial services, industrial manufacturing, utilities, healthcare, technology, and other sectors. The inputs were gathered from various locations across the Walker Information Global Network in North America, South America, the United Kingdom, Europe, and Asia and the Pacific.

The output from this database suggests that just over half of all customers (55 percent) may be *truly loyal,* indicating that they are positively engaged (i.e., have reached the Admiration gate of supplier loyalty) and that they intend to repurchase from the company.[4]

Of the remainder, one out of five (19 percent) are *high risk,* meaning they are neither pleased with nor intend to stay with their current supplier. So even many good companies (in this case, the ones that are at least investing in assessing customer feedback) can almost count on losing up to a fifth of their customers in the near term. If they don't lose these customers entirely, chances are good that, over time, the customer will seek other suppliers and use them to an increasing degree.

As if that is not bad enough, another 19 percent of current buyers feel *trapped,* which means they still plan to buy from the provider for a period of time but are not really pleased with the offering or the service. These grudging buyers may be locked in by contractual obligations or convenience, but if we do not address their relationship issues, these customers could move into the high risk category and eventually be lost for good.

Finally, 7 percent of customers are classified as being *accessible.* This means they are happy in the business relationship, like the product or service quality, but are not planning to continue the relationship and, in fact, are planning to switch in the short run. The *accessible* segment best symbolizes the urgent need to understand customer loyalty and what it really represents. Increasingly, we see buyers who switch or leave despite being perfectly satisfied. They are constantly trying new things, looking for a better business model or better ways of working with suppliers or products. We would anticipate that this customer segment will grow during chaotic technology upgrades and other business model evolutions in the twenty-first century.

If we combine the high risk and accessible categories, we see that up to 26 percent of customers say they plan to switch or leave. Why do companies face such a high degree of potential defection by customers today? There are at least three reasons:

- Customers will seek the business approach or technology they want, and there are many more options today.
- Customer expectations, as well as individual preferences, are generally on the upswing.
- Organizational growth and size hinder having close knowledge of customers.

Customers Seek What They Want— So Predict Where they Are Moving

Sometimes business leaders are shocked when clients or customers leave. But most of us, despite being satisfied customers, have changed suppliers or services to obtain something we want or just to try out a new approach. For example, many of us have ordered books or music online for less than we would have paid otherwise at a local store. Many of us will try the quick oil change near the office instead of spending more time and money at a less convenient dealer or service station.

Customers who may not leave on a whim or even in response to a good sales pitch by a competitor have fewer qualms about trying out a new approach to solve their basic need. The only countermeasure is to be ready, innovate, and understand customers well enough to provide a new approach and change the business to provide it at a profit.

We should follow the example (described in Chapter 1) of Schwab and Company, an organization remaking itself by looking ahead to ways that customers will be doing business in the future and changing the business to be the provider of the future. Put another way, if you work within the "old" business model or technology, then it doesn't matter how well you are performing because customers will still leave if another company's approach works better for them. In addition, if you are willing to evolve to new business models, there is the upside opportunity of gaining new customers who prefer the new approach.

It has definitely become harder to count on customers being loyal because the world is changing fast enough that they are open to trying new approaches that may ultimately improve their situation. It is difficult today for them even to believe in the concept of being loyal because things are changing so fast that they want to keep their options open. There are so many other competitors that it's hard to keep up with the changing expectations of customers unless a company is equipped with a system that provides regular and useful input from its customers.

If Expectations Are Rising,
Then the Way to Love Them Is to Know Them

"The only way to have a friend is to be one"
                                —Ralph Waldo Emerson.

Companies in 2000 and beyond are determined to use new technology to achieve what has been long acknowledged as a universal corporate weakness: improving the database of knowledge about customers. Just consider all the "touch-points" with customers, from point of sale to questions about usage to service. Organizations have generally not been able or willing to capture all the useful information they are given effectively, not to mention failing to be proactive about seeking and tracking customer preferences and ongoing perceptions of the value of your product versus someone else's.

A growing industry is offering software that proposes to equip firms to better capture important customer data from various touch-point sources. Despite some early-stage issues such as the technical integration across company databases and being able to update customer data easily over time, there is a great deal of hype and, more important, investment taking place in the world of customer relationship management (CRM). Some refer to these systems as "customer-centric" ones. Today CRM is "hot" because businesses recognize the challenge of maintaining customer loyalty and the cost of not doing so. Furthermore, organizations have long recognized that the caliber of their customer databases needs to be enhanced.

The principles of CRM resemble "business relationship 101"—it's all about using technology to promote active listening and other ways of understanding people to know their product preferences, shopping habits, and past complaints, not to mention their personal identification. CRM has been compared to "mom and pop" stores in small communities in an earlier era. The most successful ones kept a close watch on customers and their habits, which not only kept them on neighborly terms but helped them stock and sell more of the right things to the right customers.

Recently, I noticed that after walking into a local Jiffy Lube establishment, they "knew" me as soon as they entered my license plate number. They also "knew" my particular car: its service history, what features of service it tends to receive, and so forth. Any one of a number of their employees whom I've never met can access the database and treat me and my cars as though they know us . . . because given the right information, they do! (Jiffy Lube International bills itself as "the largest franchising organization in the rapidly expanding fast-lube industry.")[5]

Retail consumer establishments must keep tabs on large numbers of accounts with CRM, but they at least can use the point of sale as a means for entering or updating new information with all locations networked into the same database. Business-to-business relationships present a greater challenge. Each customer account has different people interacting with the various functional areas of the partner or vendor—sales, customer service, order processing, technical sales, field support—and that same matrix of interactions might be repeated in different business units or districts or even in different countries.

You can imagine the challenge of having customers in one of your national accounts feel that your representatives "know" them, when you are a multinational firm handling hundreds of large accounts worldwide and literally thousands of customer contacts who reach you through a variety of sales or service channels.

Ultimately the CRM approach attempts to integrate all areas of the business that touch the customer. CRM software seeks to improve business interactions with customers by automating the records of customer contacts; CRM also inputs the data so they can be accessed to enhance customer relationships. As more companies use CRM, customer expectations that even large organizations should "know" their customers will increase.

In addition to managing loyalty by knowing our customers' purchase histories and preferences, we must also seek their assessment of our relationship from time to time. As in any relationship, there is a time to consider the nature of how we are relating and how it can be improved. Such discussions may seem awkward because they invite criticism. Despite any discomfort, however, honest feedback is ultimately helpful.

In business we recommend that a customer relationship assessment become a regular part of your CRM system. Through either a self-administered questionnaire or a third-party interview, your strategic customers can provide you with feedback on all key aspects of the business relationship.

If Organizations Have Barriers to Knowing Customers, Then the Only Way to Really Know Them Is to Ask Them

We have been discussing how business success hinges on the ability to establish, build, and maintain relationships with customers. We have also said that in today's highly competitive environment, a satisfied customer is not necessarily a loyal customer. On the other hand, make no mistake—your chances of keeping customers increase dramatically to the degree that they are pleased or satisfied with the relationship they have with you. But there are other dynamics going on in terms of their decision making that we need to keep abreast of as well.

Implementing a CRM system is certainly one approach to staying on top of what customers appear to want based on conversations during sales or customer service calls, as well as monitoring their purchasing habits. Despite these excellent types of observations of customers and their preferences, however, we can never fully understand our customer relationships unless we ask them about it. It's not unlike the tendency to provide employees with feedback via assessments from their co-workers, commonly known as the "360-degree assessment."

Asking a customer to evaluate its relationship with your business is definitely distinguished from a simple report card–type assessment of a recent transaction, purchase, or experience. The relationship assessment asks a customer to invest more in the relationship by answering questions in a structured manner and thoughtfully assessing the supplier organization and its people. The results of these assessments, if reported effectively, can be used to augment the overall strategy and function of the company and, in the business-to-business environment, help guide individual account planning.

The effective application of feedback from customers regarding their relationships stems from understanding the elements that drive loyalty for customers within your most strategic segments of customers. In addition to measuring the relative weight that different aspects of the relationship carry in driving loyalty for customers, there is, of course, a need to understand how well each of those aspects is being performed in the customer's mind. These two components— the weight or effect of each item on loyalty and the perceived performance on the item—are combined to provide strategic direction for the organization.

The example summary report page of the customer relationship feedback for the ABC Company in Figure 5.1 reveals strategic and tactical priorities for any firm with a mission to be customer focused. It highlights what we call critical improvement areas: targets for business improvement to enhance loyalty. The critical improvements reflect where this company under-performs (at least relative to competitors), and secondary ones reflect the same with less severity.

Customer Relationship Assessment   WalkerInformation   **ABC's Summary Report**

Improvement Priorities

ABC Company's Image is a strength to leverage. Improvement priorities should focus on demonstrating value through improved coverage and benefits.

	Critical Improvements	Secondary Improvements	Leverageable Strengths
Overall Measures	Price (61%) Value (40%)	Quality (70%)	Customer-Focused Image (85%) Market Leadership Image (84%)

	Critical Improvements	Secondary Improvements	Leverageable Strengths
Experiences	Products – Easy to Use Sales Rep – Accessible Products – Ease of Installation Billing – Reasonable Time to Pay Delivery Time of Bill Sales Rep – Understanding Your Business Frequency of Contact Problem Solving Professionalism	Customer Service – Problem Resolved First Time Not on Hold Billing – Payment Flexibility Sales Rep – Being Knowledgeable Delivery – On Time Emergency Service	Customer Service – Being Courteous Answering Questions Correctly Billing – Providing Sufficient Detail Ease of Reading Bill Dispute Process

Items under each area are listed in order of impact.

Action Plans

Based on program results, the following recommended strategic priorities have been identified:

Area	Recommended Actions	Leader	Support Area	Date
Products	Conduct customer training on new product adaptations geared toward usage ease.	Technical Support	Engineering	11/97
	Determine root causes of installation difficulties. Assign task team to remedy *each* issue.	Installation Support	Engineering Service Rep	1/98
Billing	Review cash management trade-off models to see whether key assumptions can be revised.	Finance	MIS	10/97
	Identify and launch alternative payment methods such as revolving interest payment option.	Finance	Marketing	11/97
Sales Rep	Expedite purchase of communication tool upgrades (voice messaging, pagers) for Field Sales force.	Sales	Purchasing	10/97
	Expedite plans for technical, industry, and customer relations training.	Training	Marketing, HR, Sales	11/97

ABC Customer Relationship Assessment, Report Summary
©1999, Walker Information, Confidential and Proprietary
(Abc_97customds/By_TBA_Indexp.ppt 7/99 /jmh

WalkerInformation Global Network

FIGURE 5.1   ABC Customer Assessment, Report Summary.

The analysis reveals the proven competencies or leverageable strengths as well. These customer-revealed strengths help us know the recognized differentiating factors that may be under-leveraged at this point among prospective customers. These key drivers of loyalty are ones in which ABC enjoys a competitive advantage. Effective communication of these may help the firm differentiate from other brands and grow its sales volume.

....

Case in Point: Distinctive Customer and Community Relationships Under Construction

Centex Corporation of Dallas, Texas builds homes in 22 states in the United States and has begun operations in the United Kingdom and Mexico. Gaining widespread visibility has been hard to come by in an industry still largely fragmented among local builders, but the growth of Centex, combined with its corporate focus on customer satisfaction and involvement in community activities, is heightening its public exposure.

Real estate developers may not be the first firms people think of when environmental awards are handed out. But Centex Homes received the prestigious Conservation Leadership Award in November 2000, sponsored by the Nature Conservancy of Texas' Conservation Council, the Dallas *Morning News* and the Greater Dallas Chamber, in recognition of "leadership in the dedication to conserving natural resources."[6]

In 1998, Chief Executive Timothy R. Eller was also honored as "National Builder of the Year" by *Professional Builder* magazine. Eller attributes the company's success to delegating major responsibilities down to neighborhood managers, who tend to better understand the needs of local homebuyers.[7] Centex tends to serve home buyers desiring new suburban homes and neighborhood services. To help ensure that the corporation as a whole meets the wants and needs of customers, the company installed a very formal, continuous customer feedback program in 1993.

This program contacts every new homeowner shortly after the closing on the new home to complete an assessment interview or questionnaire. A third-party professional survey firm conducts telephone interviews with as many customers as can be reached. All others are mailed comparable questionnaires, and the program consistently achieves participation from about 75 percent of the new customers.

The survey questions evaluate all key aspects of the home buying and building processes, ranging from details about introducing customers to the neighborhood and model home, to construction quality, to sales representative services before and after construction. Results are reported down to the neighborhood level each quarter and up to the district, region, and an overall corporate report.

Centex backs up its commitment to customer satisfaction by tying the survey results into performance bonuses for managers from the neighborhood level and up. As a result, local managers readily make adjustments to improve results, and many hold special meetings or workshops to decide what new actions to take. The focus on improving customer scores has reached the point where many division managers are holding their field managers and sales managers accountable for achieving high ratings from the individual home buyers that they have serviced.

One early lesson from Centex customer feedback represented a surprise for managers—that achieving high customer satisfaction means managing customer expectations as much as what they actually do for them. For example, Centex surveys found new home buyers had been disappointed that the progress on their home seemed to stop for brief periods. Temporary down time on any one project is typical in home building, due to supply delivery delays or to crews finishing other projects. Yet despite the fact that the final schedule was typically not jeopardized by these temporary stoppages, the customers of Centex were uncomfortable at suddenly not seeing the crew on the job. The company has now learned to inform customers in advance of what to expect during the process, including any temporary work stoppages.

Customers felt inconvenienced more than the company realized when subcontractors arrived after the closing (often when customers were moving in or settling in) to finish some final details on the home. The impact of this information on Centex was noted by David Sasina, Senior Vice President—Marketing, who observed, "Since completing the home by the closing was found to be the number one driver of customer referrals based on the survey, that became the most important thing to our operations." Sasina adds that the customer feedback probably has achieved credibility as a corporate performance measurement tool for Centex because it benefits their business in the following three ways:

1. *Reduced warranty exposure:* Centex has long followed quality principles in building, but the high standard of customer expectations has reduced what Sasina calls PONC—the Price of Non-Conformance—when any rework is required.[8]

2. *Improved organizational productivity:* The company has evidence that using knowledge of what customers want as a priority has meant fewer complaints during the building process, thus freeing workers to build according to the plan and schedule rather than putting out fires.

3. *Increased referrals from customers*—Customer loyalty in this business hinges on the willingness of people to tell others about their builder. As Sasina says, "Referrals are a great way to drive sales."

Has higher customer satisfaction paid off in terms of business performance at Centex? David Sasina says he finds "an extraordinarily high correlation between the customer scores for divisions and the financial performance and operational levels of excellence for those same divisions."[9]

Centex Corporation continues to be recognized for its performance in this cyclical industry and for its corporate citizenship efforts. *Fortune* magazine in February 2000 named Centex Corporation number one among America's "most admired" firms in the engineering and construction category. The company won based on criteria including management caliber, financial performance, product quality, and social responsibility.[10]

. . . .

Talking to Defectors Helps Us Know the Bigger Picture for Customers

Not having direct input from your strategic customers makes it difficult to manage customer loyalty, especially with regard to understanding their expectations, as illustrated by Centex learning that they needed to alert new home owners to any building schedule in-terruptions. Actually, we can never assume we fully understand cus-tomer expectations even when they are satisfied, because as long as their options in the marketplace change, customers will never be completely satisfied. Consider

- the tendency of customers to try or adopt new "business models" (new approaches that businesses or vendors offer customers, such as Web shopping) or to try competitive products that offer new features;
- the tendency for some customers to simply tire of using the consumer brand or of the same business-to-business supplier relationship and want to make a change; and
- the customers who never admit that price is an issue, but at some point receive an offer that they simply cannot refuse.

How do we track or even anticipate such tendencies? The only way to understand the buying habits of customers thoroughly is to inter-view not only the people staying as good customers with you, *but also those who have gone or are leaving*. Not all customers are alike in profile or preferences, and there are usually some unique differ-ences between the ones who have chosen to stay with you and those who leave. Understanding those differences can be very important in understanding the direction in which market-perceived value seems to be headed.

With regard to interviewing lost customers, there are three perti-nent types of questions that need to be answered:

1. To what business model or competitor has the customer switched, and what was the attraction?
2. What deficiencies or concerns with the prior supplier contributed to the decision to switch?
3. What are the attributes, attitudes, and demographics of lost customers when compared to those who are still loyal?

The answers to the first two questions require direct questioning and careful probing. The third question requires a lengthier battery of answers about the drivers of customer loyalty and demographics and analysis that compares the data for the lost versus the loyal customers. The major differences between the two groups are likely indicators of why lost customers have moved in the direction that they have.

Tip: If lost/switched customers are hard to find or survey, then seek feedback from "partially lost" buyers, who are still with you despite reducing their purchase levels or buying more from your competitors. If they prefer another brand to yours, much can be learned by asking them to compare the two, in addition to the questions above. But at any rate, they are often more willing to cooperate in a survey because they still have a business relationship with you.

. . . .

Case in Point: A Study of Loyal and Lost Customers in Healthcare Delivery

Evaluating member loyalty is quite important for most healthcare benefit providers because loyal members provide higher profitability through lower acquisition and enrollment costs. They also tend to spread a positive message with regard to the expertise of the provider.

In this case, a projectable sample of former HMO plan members was interviewed using lost customer assessment methodology. Then the feedback from those lost customer participants was compared to similar information collected from current HMO plan members. The two sets of data were analyzed using a predictive linking model, with the key objectives of the analysis being to

- understand thoroughly why members leave and at what point they become at risk for becoming a lost customer,
- determine the degree to which attrition is preventable and the course HMOs should take to retain current members and recover lost ones, and

- develop a profile of recoverable members to help guide recovery efforts (versus unprofitable attempts aimed at the permanently lost segment).

The study findings implied that proactive behavior on the part of the HMO was very important in regard to member issues. It appeared that it would be far less expensive to keep members than to reacquire and reenroll them. Some other key findings included the following:

- There were discernible attitudinal and demographic differences between current and lost members. The differences implied that those leaving were more likely to have children under 12, thus paying higher family premiums and having more co-pays for office visits.
- A notable proportion of member loss was perceived by the HMO to be controllable because they were cases in which the employer rather than the member selected providers. This information obviously implied the need to survey the decision-makers for group accounts.
- Among the controllable reasons, cost was one of the critical reasons why the majority of members switch.
- Offering more choice in terms of doctors and hospital options was another way to help stop controllable member loss.
- We did find that more than one in four lost members were highly likely to recommend their former HMO and felt the value of the plan had been good, indicating that at least this segment was potentially recoverable and probably worth the effort of focusing marketing resources.

Armed with this type of information, the healthcare organization developed and marketed a plan to employers that had a higher concentration of member characteristics that were implied by the study. In addition, cost containment measures were enhanced to offer lower premiums to members, and there was more diligence generally toward a strategy to enjoy longer-term relationships with members.

This example suggests that assessing lost customers as well as current ones and comparing the findings is the type of customer information feedback needed in the twenty-first century.

....

The Need for Individual Account Reporting in the Twenty-First Century

The nature of customer survey research has certainly changed from the day when the standard ethic for the research industry was never to reveal the identity of individual participants in a research study. That ethic changed quickly when participants increasingly were the decision-makers in businesses or households that were involved in assessing their relationship with their supplier or service provider. In that context, and because the sponsor of the study had even provided the database of its customers to accomplish the relationship assessments, it was very appropriate to share individual account feedback with the provider. To promote openness on the part of participants, they are still typically offered an option of keeping their answers confidential. But it is interesting that in most cases, more than 90 percent of the survey participants want their provider to have their verbatim comments and recommendations rather than remaining anonymous.

This being the case, one would not want to leave out the open-ended questions and suggestion box–type probing that can provide rich feedback regarding the changing preferences and needs of decision-makers. If the survey is self-administered online or even by telephone interviewers, it is important to utilize software that can make the verbatim comments readily available (virtually in real time) so that the people in the organization responsible for those accounts are armed with their customers' assessments as quickly as possible. Sometimes a third-party assessment may uncover problems that otherwise hadn't been complained about, or even intentions to try competitive offerings that hadn't been shared with the customer's account person. This database of comments can become part of the

CRM or be handled as a separate database, but the important thing is that it provides access to those who need to know the true feelings of the clients they are responsible for.

Examples of business-to-business questions that produce useful verbatim feedback follow:

- Considering all that (SUPPLIER NAME) provides, what do you and your colleagues want them to improve first or add to what they deliver?
- What has occurred in the recent past that you or your colleagues have considered to be a problem with (SUPPLIER NAME)'s service or deliverables?
- Looking ahead at least two years, what are some of your firm's changing needs, and how might those changes require (SUPPLIER NAME) to adjust what they provide in the relationship?
- What has (SUPPLIER NAME) done for your firm in the past year that you consider helpful or positive to the point of strengthening the business relationship?

Using Customer Information to Drive Change in the Organization

There are two levels of action based on customer feedback information. One is at the account level, where feedback to both the closed and open-ended questions immediately enables account teams to solve client problems and enables higher levels of management to prepare strategic account plans. The NCR Corporation case in point in this chapter details how such a program is being used by a leading global organization.

The second type of action planning is with the aggregate customer findings that show either common issues or potential strategic weaknesses from the perspective of customers. These types of commonly held issues are ideally addressed by special teams pulled together from across the organization that are empowered to design and implement new projects or initiatives to address them.

Obviously, without taking action the primary benefit of having customer assessment information is lost. Knowledge can be useless unless it drives decisions in the form of new projects, new communications/messages, or new strategies undertaken to improve the business.

The first step in effectively integrating customer assessment feedback at a corporate level is to obtain senior-level endorsement of that effort. There must be a champion at the highest level possible for any new initiatives to be adequately supported and equipped or staffed.

The second step is to identify leaders of initiatives in different teams or functional areas of the company, based on customer feedback priorities. Put another way, ask any pertinent functional or team leaders in the organization to define what major initiative needs to be undertaken based on the results of the customer assessment.

The third general step then becomes using generally accepted project management techniques in your own corporate culture to ensure that each of those initiatives is approved and undertaken. As an example, consider a case where customer feedback indicated a critical need to enhance the response time for connecting customer service representatives with the customers calling in while minimizing the amount of hold time. Assume also that in the same functional area there were customer concerns about the service representatives' knowledge of the customer's service history.

These two priority concerns in the customer service operation could trigger two separate initiatives: a reevaluation of the automatic call answering system with the specific goal of enhancing the connect time with a service representative, and an assessment of the customer service database system so that customer histories are more readily available to service representatives when the customer calls come in. For each of the two initiatives, a project leader and improvement team members would be assigned, target dates to submit a proposal for the recommendations would be established, and other project initiatives unique to the planning cycle of the organization would be identified.

There are a few important points to remember regarding this type of action planning and use of customer information:

- Don't try to change too many issues at one time. It usually works better for any organization to only take on two to four priority projects simultaneously.
- Do keep senior managers involved as champions behind each project.
- Do establish a system of accountability for the teams in terms of the type of proposal expected and the timing of publishing it.
- Do plan to use whatever project or team approach already exists in your culture for addressing new initiatives.
- Don't assume that the initiatives can be resolved in just one or two meetings. There are actually two phases for a team (or two different teams): confirm what the problem is and propose a new process or system, then implement any approved change or new system.

We normally recommend a 10-step process for action planning and implementation of customer information because some process or system issues (in addition to individual account solutions) usually are uncovered:

1. Establish a cross-functional or steering implementation team.
2. Agree on customer priorities.
3. Determine the reasons for customer priorities, that is, any current initiatives that are related to those priorities or other contributing elements to those issues.
4. Identify key areas of focus for action.
5. Assign project teams for each initiative.
6. Charge project teams with developing detailed action plans or proposals for any new systems.
7. Approve and finalize detailed plans.
8. Implement plans.

9. Monitor progress on implementation.
10. Reassess customer perceptions post-implementation.

Remember that for business-to-business organizations there are basically two levels of information available with customer relationship feedback: strategic, meaning in this case cross-functional or corporate-wide customer priorities; and tactical, meaning customer issues that are local or account-specific. Your organization must be prepared to act on both types of input to make your information program investment worthwhile.

The guidelines just presented apply mainly to the strategic implications received from customer survey data, analyzed to reflect corporate strengths and weaknesses. Cross-functional initiatives are launched to address those issues, and this information is used as well during the regular planning process. An example of this is the company seeking to enhance the connect time to customer service representatives, described previously.

In service businesses and business-to-business situations, equal attention must be given to the feedback from individual customers. Customer decision-makers will offer concerns, describe competitive offerings, and even pay compliments in a self-administered assessment or one conducted by a third-party interviewer. In many cases, this will be information that otherwise would not be shared in the course of the business relationship, or at least not be entered into your customer information system. Armed with this valuable feedback, account teams can integrate it into their account servicing and plan solutions and longer-term account strategies.

Say for example that Rachel, a high-performing national accounts manager, knows that her biggest customer, Acme Industries, has a few concerns about lead times for product delivery. She has stayed in touch with her main customer contact on this issue and personally helped solve a scheduling problem or two in the previous six months. But then the annual customer assessment survey results for the Acme account come in, and she not only confirms that her contacts at Acme are concerned about the scheduling lead times with her firm, she hears for the first time that some people there are in the beginning stages of switching some of their business to a leading competitor based on promises of special discount pricing with higher-volume ordering.

This new information provides tangible evidence to help Rachel inspire urgency and get her team to adjust service delivery, negotiate pricing if necessary, and secure this important account. Armed with the survey responses, she also holds meetings with the client to explore issues further. She then returns with more detail for action and convinces her management to invest in the necessary adjustments in the contract and the service commitments.

Another example using customer feedback tactically is when large consumer service organizations, such as utilities, financial institutions, or home services, find wide differences in customer "scores" from local districts or offices. As in the case of Centex Homes, the local office manager should be given incentives to know the local market well enough to offer the right products and service delivery to his or her customers.

Rules of thumb for customer relationship assessment systems are to use them to

- consider better customer communications and expectations management in all key markets, including the lost or partially lost customers;
- initiate improvement projects for improved delivery of product or service solutions; and
- integrate local or even account-level feedback into servicing and supporting those customers.

What is the next frontier for customer assessment programs? Leading companies are already using technology that more smoothly integrates customer survey assessment data into a system allowing results and follow-up action planning to be more widely communicated through the organization. Eventually we will see customer assessment data become an integral part of CRM systems. While this type of software is evolving, companies will increasingly use technology to at least disseminate the learning from the customer assessments. The following case study illustrates how even global customer feedback information and follow-up plans can be addressed by using technology effectively.

···

Case in Point: NCR Corporation

The history of Dayton, Ohio–based NCR Corporation can be summed up by saying that the firm that once mainly wanted to take people's money (via cash registers, when they were known as National Cash Register is now a leading maker of automatic teller machines (ATMs), and seeks to give people back their money. In addition to ATMs, NCR develops store automation and merchandising, or point-of-sale, systems and equipment; media products such as paper and ink; data gathering and analysis for distribution channels; and data warehousing for national/multinational accounts such as Wal-Mart and the U.S. Postal Service.

The cash register heritage of NCR dates back to 1882, when founder John Patterson purchased control of a Dayton cash register factory and, in a few years, brought in Colonel Edward Deeds (later the Chairman), and Charles Kettering, an inventor who developed the first electric cash register for NCR.

By the 1920s, NCR not only controlled 90 percent of the cash register market but had introduced accounting machines as its next major product line. NCR acquired computer technology as early as 1952 and continued developing its data processing expertise. But it did not fully automate its retail and banking product lines until the early 1970s, when new CEO William Anderson restructured the firm around ATMs and retail scanners. NCR enhanced its computer technology and networking capabilities throughout the 1980s and was purchased in a hostile takeover by AT&T in 1991. AT&T had long desired to expand into the computer business in addition to telecommunications, and felt that NCR had the right competencies and synergies to help it become a top maker of PCs.

As do so many corporate "marriages," this merger proved to be neither fulfilling nor long-lasting. According to Stephen Wall and Shannon Wall in *The Morning After,* AT&T may have been interested to learn the computer business from NCR, but they also put much energy into imposing their culture, "trying to make (NCR) just like AT&T."[11] NCR managers, coming from a more traditional culture than AT&T's, were so put off at one point by the new AT&T-prescribed titles such as "associate," "coach," or "head coach" that they responded by printing separate sets of business cards with their old titles to use with customers.

As the company piled up financial losses (ultimately totaling $4 billion) during the AT&T era, NCR was spun off in 1996. Lars Nyberg, who had been leading the business unit since being hired from Phillips in 1995, is still the CEO of NCR at this writing. He refocused the firm on its core competencies of ATMs, retail automation, data processing, and warehousing, as well as leading the company through a painful but, by most accounts, necessary restructuring. By concentrating more on the software and services components of its business, NCR has today successfully transformed itself from a hardware-only company to a $6.5 billion global business solutions provider.

NCR is committed to stakeholder measurement and uses the results of survey-based customer relationship measures to help guide its corporate strategies and management processes. NCR sets goals based on customer feedback as one means of measuring performance and conducts frequent employee and customer surveys to inspire operational and service improvement.[12]

The Customer Measurement Program

NCR obtains survey feedback from its financial services clientele, retail services, and national/global account segments in as many as 57 countries twice each year. These surveys have become a critical part of NCR's scorecard of business metrics, with each major business unit setting goals for performance and improvement.

Data collection methodology varies by country and local business culture and includes telephone interviewing, self-administered mail, and personal interviewing. Based on its global experience, the survey consulting firm uses the most appropriate approach for each country and administers the survey in the native language.

Centralizing Customer Information Management

The chronic challenge of collecting field inputs to update a customer database was further pushed at NCR to allow the surveys to be done. NCR decided to develop (with the help of their consulting firm) an Internet-based customer information management system to help NCR account managers maintain and update account-specific information.

This electronic warehouse of customer data, residing in a database managed by the outside consultant but giving online access to NCR, contains information for the accounts representing the top 80 percent of revenue for the firm; this includes all the major accounts in the financial industry and retail industry, plus NCR's data processing/warehousing customers in other industries such as telecommunications and transportation. The information includes current customer decision-makers, customer telephone numbers and addresses, type of product or solution, current NCR account team members, and other customer-specific data.

There is an attempt each year to obtain customer feedback from all accounts in the geographic market areas within each of the major NCR business units. Beyond efficient survey sampling, moving to a centralized database allowed for linking survey results with the account information, so the updated information about current account contacts was enhanced by including the detailed evaluations of those same individuals regarding their satisfaction with NCR.

As account data (e.g., new contacts, phone numbers) change, NCR account managers can access the system—available around the clock and from any Web browser—and make the necessary revisions.

Zero Cycle Time Processing and Real-Time Reporting

Despite the size and global scope of the measurement program, NCR requires timely information for its sales or account organization and other users. Survey data collection periods are at least six weeks long to ensure the greatest customer participation. This time span also helps minimize the impact of singular events in major markets, such as a transportation strike affecting all shipping or the announcement of a price increase in a product line. A standard core of questions is used in the customer contact surveys, although each major NCR business unit can add appropriate questions as needed.

Whereas most research programs wait to process findings until after all data have been collected and checked, NCR makes its findings available online even as interviews are being completed. Initial deliverables include

tabulated results by business unit, location, and other customer segments;
customer verbatim comment reports;
individual response detail reports; and
grouped response detail reports.

In business-to-business relationship markets such as NCR's, customer satisfaction in a sense only happens one account at a time. So in addition to aggregated customer feedback scores, NCR emphasizes the survey results from individual customers and accounts. Account-level customer feedback is shared with account directors within 10 days of the interview, a significant improvement over the previous survey process (prior to Internet reporting), which took as long as 10 weeks.

Thus, NCR account directors evaluate the ratings and comments of their accounts within a week or so of the customer's participation in the survey, even though some comments come from remote spots on the globe and require translation into English from 24 native languages. These users of the survey data realize that all the survey results for an account or business unit are not complete until the end of data collection, but they can see their "scores" developing as these initial reports are updated with new data each week.

Promoting Effective Follow-up to Customer Issues

Weekly posting of completed surveys allows NCR representatives to begin addressing any account issues immediately, and it also speeds up their response to emerging issues or problems revealed by the study. Follow-up meetings and improvement activities are tracked on the same system, which prompts the account managers to enter specifics about account follow-up plans, dates for planned activities, or additional information gained from the survey. Accounts considered "vulnerable" because their survey scores drop below a certain level are highlighted and can be identified and tracked separately from nonvulnerable accounts.

Senior account managers at NCR check individual accounts for the status of follow-up activities. NCR policy now requires corrective action plans for any accounts shown to be vulnerable based on the survey analysis. The tracking system makes it easy to enforce and comply with this policy.

New Expectations Bring New Features

Realities in the NCR culture now include remarkable cycle time—in posting survey results, in making the survey feedback accessible to account management, and by providing online tools for account planning. Such features have injected a new urgency into account relationship management and a new vigor into NCR's ability to meet its customers' needs. NCR has also received early indications that follow-up activities driven by these surveys improve individual customer loyalty and sales.

Additionally, this approach to account management has raised the bar on the ultimate purpose and design of customer relationship survey programs. Such programs in the past were used as a "report card" on customer satisfaction and as indicators of how to target the improvement of business processes important to customers. But this program provides even more: new guidance for decisions regarding individual customers and account relationships. Today, NCR account managers' access to performance data at an account level provides a tactical agility that makes their individual customers the immediate beneficiaries of the program, no matter where they are on the globe.[13]

From the Inside Out

The NCR case study tells a remarkable story of integrating customer feedback into a corporate culture using technological advances. But we should not lose sight of the fact that the real conduit for customer relationships is having a culture with people focused on the customer, cooperating together, and working hard toward a common purpose. Customer loyalty cannot fully develop unless an organization has great commitment from its employees. In the next chapter, we explore what a focus on employee commitment requires from business leaders today.

The Power of Employees

A number of factors have resulted in a different mind-set today among workers regarding whom they might want to work for, for how long they might want to work for anyone, and what the environment at work should be like. Long ago in the world of work, these weren't even issues. But before we get carried away complaining about the good old days, remember one truth: We did this to ourselves.

You would think we would learn. Everyone knows that business leaders during the Industrial Revolution and on into the twentieth century took their workers for granted, knowing they could be replaced from the influx who were seeking wages in the growing cities and towns. Partly as a result of this attitude, business leaders eventually wound up working not only with employees but with union organizers and union stewards as well.

Over time, life improved in the working world. In the latter half of the twentieth century, with a booming post-war economy and improved compensation and working conditions for employees, the era of the bargaining employee began to fade. The increasing number of white-collar workers settled into a working arrangement that didn't seem to require third-party union representation.

But in the recession of the 1970s and again during the era of the service economy and the rise of the global/new economy in the 1980s and 1990s, business leaders again took for granted the value of employees. Companies downsized sometimes by the thousands, first the blue-collar workforce, then the ranks of white-collar workers and middle management. Once again business leaders found themselves working with not just employees, but their agents. Only this time, many employees will become free agents along the lines of professional athletes who, after putting in their contractual time (or something less than that) for one employer, are more than ready to join another team and answer the call of the highest bidder. And there will be third-party agents (commonly called lawyers) negotiating the contracts and compensation of the more highly skilled and experienced among the workers.

Out of the Downsizing Darkness. . .

It is always a mistake to operate as if employees are dispensable or easily interchangeable, because they are not. By definition, we cannot have an organization without the right employees—people who fit our cultures, who bring the right combination of talent, experience, and personality to our organizations. These people are never easily replaced. Further, how humanely they are treated when they leave has a lasting impact on those who stay. It certainly sends a clear message about the company's commitment to workers.

Some of the risk must be clear to intelligent managers considering making reductions in staff. So why do they do it? An economic recession, then the advent of frequent mergers and acquisitions compounded by increased global competition, compelled many companies in the last part of the twentieth century to become leaner as a defensive strategy. And remember that CEOs are a competitive lot! When some firms make news by taking aggressive steps to increase profits and shareholder value, it poses a challenge to other leaders. Trusted staff or consultants present short-term ways to boost earnings and market capitalization through process improvements and staff reductions, and many leaders are already primed to do so by seeing others address the same issue in the same way.

It's not that there were not good business reasons for reengineering, outsourcing, or centralizing (sharing) support services, such as payroll. Good business management means always looking for cost reductions, especially in a crisis or when other avenues to profit growth have dried up. But "reducing head count," a term that still gets bantered about, sounds more like the management of livestock rather than people. And making a reduction in force (RIF) has long been a too-convenient balancing of the ledger to counter the past sins of poor strategy, implementation, and/or fiscal management.

Top executives then made things much worse. What kind of reaction do we expect when the cost savings from downsizing appear to employees to be just a move to boost profits rather than a last resort against serious economic trouble? Life at work can't always be democratic, but transferring value from the employees to the stock price and the incentives of the senior managers will be seen as unfair by the majority of workers in a free society.

Employees of organizations whose leaders took golden parachutes, cashed in enriched stock options, or received major bonus or salary increases following layoffs will not soon forget the experience. The natural response will be to protect themselves better in the future and tell everyone who will listen to do the same. Peter Drucker made a similar observation in a *Forbes* interview in 1997: "Few top executives can even imagine the hatred, contempt and fury that has been created—not primarily among blue-collar workers who never had an exalted opinion of the 'bosses'—but among their middle management and professional people. I don't know what form it will take, but the envy developing from (the top 'executives') enormous wealth will cause trouble."[1]

Whether they become "free agents" or simply follow the advice of many business analysts and proactively manage their own careers, people will adapt to the new environment. Whereas employers previously brought certain protections and security to jobs and careers, now employees feel they must take care of themselves. They will negotiate harder to get more, and they will promise less in terms of long-term loyalty.

Hopefully the era of large-scale indiscriminate layoffs is over. But given human imperfection, and with limits to accurately forecasting all possibilities and trends in different purchasing habits, new technologies, or down cycles, free markets will always experience cases of forced layoffs. Dot.com firms are an example today, as that category begins to shake out in the push by investors and capital markets to make them profitable.

So the lessons of downsizing must be heeded. We can set aside the more human aspects of the issue for a moment and still question the efficacy of the practice. First, take corporate performance and the downsizing strategy. Mentioned earlier was the point by Gertz and Baptista that cost-cutting organizations have generally not experienced growth following downsizing to the same degree as organizations using a different strategy. The profitable, growing firms that the Fortune 1,000 identified from 1988 to 1993 were those that had profitable growth during the period just prior. Only 7 percent of the profitable, growing firms had been cost-cutters. The authors concluded that, "The transition from cost-cutting to growth is apparently a very difficult one."[2]

It is apparently difficult even to achieve the short-term goals of cost-cutting projects that affect so many people's lives and their outlooks on the employment relationship. Authors and management consultants Terrence Deal and Allan Kennedy report in *The New Corporate Cultures* that "as many as 50% to 75% of re-engineering projects failed to achieve their goals or even positive improvements in performance." They also note that one of the fathers of reengineering, James Champy, himself admitted that restructuring projects studied by his consulting firm failed to hit their financial targets.[3]

It is a bitter irony that companies failed to hit targets or even obtain long-term growth from restructuring because the costs of it went beyond the one-time write-offs for restructuring. Individuals, their families, and the local economies experienced disruption in their lives at the least, and in many cases real suffering following permanent layoffs. The higher age and position levels usually made it impossible to find equivalent jobs after the layoffs. For most, the search went on for months. Many settled for positions with less salary, fewer benefits, or both.

The other hidden cost of downsizing is the damage done to the remaining organization in terms of the work life and morale of employees. Over time, it's true that employees in "flatter" organizations may appreciate their greater autonomy. But no matter how streamlined the processes became through reengineering at its best, there usually seemed to be more work for the fewer remaining employees. Beyond the blow to morale, many lost close friends and/or mentors. Deal and Kennedy make the interesting point that when long-term employees are let go, we lose the people who best communicate the folklore and the cultural values of the organization, because they have experienced those over time and in various situations. Corporate cultures wind up damaging themselves by suddenly removing the people who hand down the company's cultural values and its "heritage."[4]

Of course, continuing to believe in corporate values can become moot when a company decides to downsize. Depending on the organization and the situation, it can be tough to maintain a unified belief in the core principles of the firm at the same time that you are cutting a portion of the workforce.

For example, employees would have a difficult time squaring up their company's tenet of "integrity" when long-term fellow employees are being terminated for reasons unrelated to individual performance. It helps, of course, when the CEO and other leaders do a particularly effective job of communicating throughout the process why the layoff has to occur and when generous severance packages are offered. But most "right-sizings" (the newer, sanctified term for layoffs) fail to come off as being right.

For employees, we now know that perceptions of corporate integrity begin "at home," meaning in the way the company treats its employees. For evidence of worker sensitivity to this issue, consider that in a 1999 Walker Information study of U.S. employee perceptions of integrity, "unfair treatment of employees by management" was the highest-occurring "ethical violation," cited more often than sexual harassment, lying on reports, or any of a longer list of potential unethical practices.[5] For employees to buy into your corporate tenet of integrity, they will first have to see it in the relationship the company has with its associates.

This reality echoes the truth that good relationships are grounded in mutual trust. Corporate values will ring hollow to workers who have witnessed what they believe has been unfair treatment of colleagues. In fact, many have come to expect a new reality or arrangement between employer and employee that mutually assumes a more tenuous, short-term relationship than before.

Let's Make a (New) Deal

Beyond disrupting lives and core values, the downsizing era had a permanent impact on the traditional unwritten contract for employee loyalty. It loosened the bonds between employee and employer, with people today bringing a different attitude to their work and their careers.

The traditional relationship was for the employee to work hard and consistently, expecting in return security and long-term employment, if not a job for life. The new arrangement still evolving has been termed the "new deal"—one that is clearly a different mutual understanding of what the employment "contract" will be.

A new employment arrangement is evolving that will offer benefits to both businesses and employees, although both must work to rebuild the sense of relationship and recapture some of the old spirit of mutual cooperation. One of the best terms I have come across to describe the new contract between employer and employee is "conscious loyalty," coined by Cliff Hakim, President of Rethinking Work and contributor to a Conference Board paper on new employment relationships.[6] "Conscious" is more apt a description than "blind" loyalty. Although people were never really blind to their ultimate responsibility and potential vulnerability as employees, they have become much more conscious of their dependency and insecurity given the turbulent events taking place in the world and in business cycles. Being conscious implies being ready for what might happen, but also looking for opportunities in every work situation.

Employees today are also saying that "if you're not guaranteeing me a job, at least help me become more marketable during the time I spend with you." People now expect to be trained and equipped reasonably during their tenure with an organization, not only to do their jobs better but to make themselves more effective in managing their careers going forward. This definitely is being conscious and yet reasonable, given today's market conditions.

What do employees expect to learn beyond job skills and functional knowledge? For one thing, they want to be plugged into the vision of the firm, and they want to share in the understanding of where their company fits into its market channels and into the future. They also want to know where their job fits into the company and how it complements the goals of the company.

The new deal or the new arrangement with employees is not exactly the complete opposite of blind loyalty. Employees may no longer completely depend on their employers, but at the same time they haven't become totally independent, either. There will be some "free agents" among the very highest or most uniquely skilled workers. The new deal is truly something in between—call it "interdependence," or again, "conscious loyalty."

One of the challenges remaining in the new relationship is how to regain lost trust. Relationships require a foundation of trust. Employees can be reassured by witnessing management take actions that show honest concern for people. These are not new value statements, but rather business decisions that account for the wants and needs of employees. Leaders also owe it to employees to establish a vision for the firm and to explain that vision in terms of how the company is dealing with migrations of value in the marketplace that mean their companies must change accordingly.

One description of the "new deal" in the Conference Board report was given by Patricia Milligan, Principal of Towers Perrin:

If employees:
- develop skills that they need
- apply them to help the company win
- live out the corporate values

And if the company provides:
- a challenging work environment
- support for the development of the individual
- appropriate rewards for their contribution

Then both sides are part of a revitalized industry leader.[7]

....

Case in Point: United Parcel Service and the New Loyalty Contract with Employees

United Parcel Service is the world's largest express carrier and package delivery company. At the time that CEO James Kelly delivered his keynote talk at the Human Resource Planning Society's annual conference in March 1998, UPS was the nation's third-largest employer, and it currently has approximately 342,000 employees in its global workforce. This firm's ideas regarding employee relationship management are worth considering, particularly given that (in Kelly's words), UPS "virtually never had to consider long-term or permanent layoffs."[8]

UPS weathered a major strike in 1997 by the Teamsters, who had long wanted to see UPS provide more full-time jobs with benefits (package loaders have traditionally been part-time). The strike lasted 15 days, costing the company hundreds of millions of dollars, and was settled by integrating part-time jobs into some 10,000 new full-time positions. Another strike was avoided the following year when UPS pilots were given five-year contracts with pay raises. Kelly's perspective about employee loyalty has been wrought from experience, including labor pressures along with other forms of employee dialogue. But UPS has gone on record as not only listening to its associates but also making major adjustments to accommodate workers without losing sight of other business goals.

So what is UPS's take on the new employee/employer arrangement? First, Kelly's passion regarding the importance of employees becomes clear when he quoted the Sloan Management Study linking employee loyalty to organizational performance. Kelly said that a metric of employee loyalty "deserves a place on the balance sheet, right next to other key assets."[9] He then went on to recognize the new reality of employee loyalty today by stating what the employer side must be. What hasn't changed is that employers have to make a "realistic commitment to the long haul" for the sake of employees by:

1. Giving employees some stake (ownership) in the business as a motivator as well as a reward. (UPS went public in 1999, but management, employees, retirees, and the founding families continue to own 90 percent of the stock.)[10]
2. Offering flexible career paths for the longer-term employees. Internal job postings and opportunities span the many UPS locations and business units. Workers at entry level and higher responsibilities are encouraged to apply for other jobs. Managers expect to be offered other functional jobs to round out their experience.
3. Emphasizing promotion from within to leverage the proven value and knowledge of employees as well as to provide them with further motivation to stay. UPS's website claims, "Every member of the senior management team began their careers at the front lines of the company as package sorters, drivers and administrative assistants."[11]

The second major deliverable to employees for building the new relationship is what Kelly called the "career toolbox," which includes:

1. Ongoing professional training extending well beyond orientation to ensure professional development at each new job and stage of a career—over $300 million spent per year in employee learning programs;
2. Effective performance evaluation and reward systems that directly counter political favoritism;
3. Rewarding managers for more than just direct performance through a more balanced measurement system. At UPS this includes measures that are financially driven, productivity-driven, and people-driven (how performance has affected customers and colleagues/coworkers).[12]

Kelly then spoke to the employee side of the new employment equation and interestingly emphasized one major concept: flexibility. Employees are simply expected to be more flexible in:

- Managing their own careers, even if they stay with UPS. Employees must take initiative in picking up the tools they are offered and making effective use of them.
- Realizing that strong performance will be continually expected on their part in whatever job they are currently assigned.[13]

Kelly made two strong recommendations to business leaders based on his experience at UPS:

1. Don't overlook the hidden loyalty still existing in the hearts and minds of employees today. He cited cases at UPS and elsewhere proving that many employees still have a heart for their organization as long as a sense of trust exists.
2. He repeatedly emphasized the value of using employee loyalty and satisfaction as a key metric in managing the organization. UPS has made the connections in its district performance between higher employee satisfaction and higher productivity.[14]

The Coming Era of Employee Value

The saga of the employee as a corporate stakeholder will continue to unfold in the twenty-first century as long as the economic boom continues. The story line has had many twists and turns, but certain implications are becoming clearer: The pendulum is shifting from workers being thought of as expendable during the past twenty years to workers becoming virtually indispensable today. This evolution is especially true for higher-skilled workers, although employee retention efforts are increasingly focused on minimum-wage staff as well.

Profitability, along with shareholder value, are never out of vogue as the ultimate definitions of business success. But the notion of cutting labor to the bone as the approach for increasing shareholder value, beautifying the corporate balance sheet, and driving up stock value in the short run has hopefully been exposed as shortsighted if not unethical. Stock and market values can be successfully built within boundaries of fair play and with the support of employees.

It certainly didn't take very long for the pendulum of employee value to begin swinging back. A 1998 Lou Harris survey among U.S. CEOs of large companies ($100 million and over) indicated that three-fourths of the CEOs anticipate employees will be a more critical stakeholder than ever to their organizations in the near future, and only 4 percent thought they would be any less important.[15]

So Where Are Those Skilled Employees When We Need Them?

One reason the value of workers is rising is that there are not enough of them to go around, and that trend will probably get worse. A number of dynamics were presented at the beginning of this book suggesting that the United States—and ultimately much of the world economy—may be in for a reasonably lengthy economic boom. An outgrowth of that prospering economy has been a low unemployment rate.

The rate of unemployment among the developed member countries of the OECD was 6.6 percent in February 2000, 0.4 percentage points lower than just a year earlier. This rate was down from 7.4 percent as recently as 1997 and from over 8 percent as recently as 1994. Unemployment for the United States has hovered around 4 percent since mid-1999, down from 4.9 percent in 1997 and a high of about 8 percent in 1992. For the record, four countries have sustained double digit unemployment rates since 1997: Finland, France, Italy, and Spain. As a whole, however, the European countries' unemployment has been slowly dropping since 1997.[16]

Proof That They Are Not Staying

Especially in the United States, it has never been more challenging to find skilled workers and, in turn, to keep them once they are found. Figures available from the Bureau of National Affairs survey of employee turnover suggest that employee turnover as of the end of 1999 had hit its highest level in two decades. (See Figure 6.1.) The rate of "permanent separations," which exclude layoffs, reductions in force, and departures of temporary staff, averaged 14.4 percent annually in 1998 (1.2 percent monthly average). This rate was up slightly over the previous two years and is notably higher than the 10.8 percent reported as recently as 1996. It also is the highest 12-month average recorded since 1981.[17]

The median number of years that both wage and salary workers are staying with their current employer peaked in 1996 at 3.8 and has since dropped steadily, to 3.5 in 2000, which is back to where it stood in the mid-1980s, according to U.S. labor statistics.[18] Employee tenure data vary dramatically by industry sector, as illustrated in Figure 6.2. Certain industries' employees keep their workers well over the norm of three to four years, such as the government (over seven years), communications, and manufacturing (both over five years). At the other extreme, retail stands out with its relatively brief average tenure of just two years.

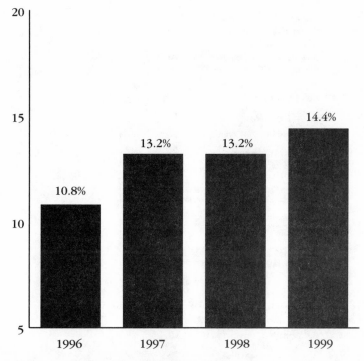

FIGURE 6.1   Annual Employee Turnover Rates.
Source:Adapted from The Bureau of National Affairs, Inc., "Economy Spurs
Highest Turnover Rates In Nearly 20 Years, BNA survey Finds" (press release),
http://www.bna.com/press/pr00.htm (March 13, 2000)

Beyond the differences in the length of tenure, the trends in average tenure vary by industry as well. Government, with employees
having the longest tenure among sectors, is still growing in average
tenure. Health services tended to have below-average tenure, but the
time spent with current employers is growing in that sector. In contrast, the median tenure of communications employees has been cut
in half in less than a decade, from a median of almost ten years to just
over five years today. Tenure in the transportation sector appears to
be falling off notably as well.

Another reality that is approaching is the peaking of the size of the
U.S. workforce. Richard W. Judy, Senior Fellow of the Hudson Institute
and President, Hudson Analytics, predicts from the U.S. government
data that by the year 2016, there will be a net decrease in the U.S.

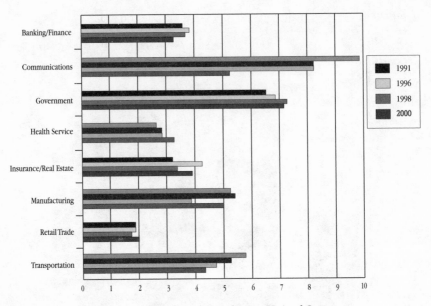

FIGURE 6.2   Employment Tenure by Industry, United States
Source: Bureau of Labor Satistics, "Labor Statistics from the Current Population
Survey," http://stats.bls.gov/newsrels.htm.

workforce for the first time ever because of the combination of slow
population growth and the retirement of baby-boomers. Judy adds
that national immigration policy changes are the only likely "wild
card" that could noticeably change this prediction, because all future
U.S. workers have been born and accounted for.[19]

Despite the continued loss of blue-collar positions, including opera-
tors, fabricators, and laborers, the Hudson Institute book *Workforce
2020* predicts a shortage in "local services" jobs that may drive up the
wages for those types of positions. These include health and social
workers. On the other hand, several occupations growing the most
rapidly are not the low-paying ones, but the ones paying the best,
which puts even greater pressure on business leaders to reconsider
what the employment contract needs to be and to plan on rebuilding
relationships with employees. Hudson used Bureau of Labor projections to rank the occupations growing the fastest between the years
1994 and 2005. As shown in Table 6.1, the list includes local services

TABLE 6.1   The 25 Fastest-Growing Occupations, 1994–2005*

Occupation**	Net Job Growth (Thousands)	Percent Change in Employment
Personal and homecare aides	212	188
Home health aides	428	102
Systems analysts	445	92
Computer engineers	177	91
All other computer scientists	134	90
Physical therapists	81	79
Residential counselors	125	76
Human services workers	125	74
Medical assistants	121	59
Paralegals	65	59

* As projected by the Bureau of Labor Statistics
** Only occupations with at least 100,000 employees in 1994 are included.
Source: Richard W. Judy and Carol D'Amico, *Workforce 2020: Work and Worker in the 21st Century* (Indianapolis: Hudson Institute, 1998), 78.

but also highly skilled job categories, such as systems analysts, computer engineers, and physical therapists.[20]

The Economics of Supply Shortages

A survey of 203 leaders in businesses with 10 to 500 employees indicates that start-ups and other small businesses are already experiencing hiring challenges. The study, by Sage Software, reported in *Industry Week* that 37 percent of small businesses are having trouble recruiting the workers needed, and that over half now use the Internet in their recruiting efforts. Nearly half were offering higher-than-ever salaries plus incentives for referrals; 28 percent said they had been pushed to increase salaries dramatically to keep current employees by matching increased market values.[21]

The study sponsor commented on the changed employment atmosphere: "Interviewees have become the interviewers, questioning recruiters about workplace environment, stock options, bonus plans, child-care availability, and creative scheduling. Recruiters have to know what potential employees are looking for, and then be flexible and creative."[22]

One way employers have adapted has been to sweeten the pot of benefits for associates. In 1984, when Robert Levering and Milton Moskowitz first published their list of "The 100 Best Companies to Work For," only one offered on-site daycare. According to the newest list reported in the January 2000 issue of *Fortune*, 29 of the top 100 companies now provide daycare. In 1984, only two of the companies (Federal Express and Northwestern Mutual Life) offered employees flexible (flextime) schedules; now 70 do. Following are some of the other benefits offered by the top 100 firms:

- Thirty-six of the 58 publicly held firms on the list offer stock options to all their employees.
- Fifty-three firms provide on-site university courses; 91 have tuition reimbursement, with 24 reimbursing more than $4,000 per year.
- Forty-five firms offer reduced summer hours.
- Seventy-two firms have job sharing options available.
- Eighty-seven firms offer telecommuting positions.
- A compressed workweek schedule is offered by 89 firms.[23]

Compensation, whether in the form of benefits, salary, or incentives, will certainly be an important consideration for employees who are considering career changes and offers. At the same time, it certainly helps to stay abreast of what else really matters to workers. The last four benefits listed above offer job flexibility rather than traditional perks, symbolizing how employee priorities are changing.

There will always be limits to what can be offered in employee compensation, benefits, and policies. Michael O'Malley, an employment expert with William Mercer, the management consultancy, has suggested that becoming fixated with always making the best offers can result in "a 'deal' culture where everything is for sale and every-thing can be bargained."[24]

On the other hand, the ultimate cost to avoid may be the price of employee turnover. According to *The Economist* in a July 2000 story about U.S. employee turnover, the cost of employee churn has been estimated by most analysts to be 1.5 times the employee's salary. Even the cost of replacing a worker in the ostensibly more replaceable fast food category is more than $500. At the other end of the spectrum (aside from executives) are software engineers, where the total cost of leaving (including lost production time and recruiting and training the replacement) could exceed $100,000.[25] These estimates may sound high until we consider the full costs not only of recruiting new workers, but training, loss of productivity, and other hidden costs, as seen in the checklist that follows.

Turnover Cost Elements

Hard Costs.

- Separation processing
- Co-worker overtime/added shifts
- Headhunter/search costs
- Cost of developing advertising and buying ad space
- Selection and orientation costs (interviewing, background checks/testing, orientation, and on-the-job training)

Soft Costs.

- Pre-departure inefficiency costs (reduced productivity of employee, co-workers, and supervisor)
- During vacancy inefficiency costs (lost productivity with vacant position and supervisor filling in)
- Selection and orientation inefficiency costs (lost productivity of employee, co-workers, and supervisor during training)[26]

The State of Employee Loyalty

When a stringent measure of loyalty is applied, employers might be somewhat shocked at how few truly loyal associates they have today. The 1999 Employee Relationship Report benchmark study by Walker Information and Hudson Institute included 2,293 responses from employees representing business, government, and nonprofit employers with 50 or more employees in the United States. Highlighting its results will lend understanding to the elements that will be needed for employers to strengthen their relationships with employees. It may also serve as a wake-up call regarding the seriousness of certain loyalty issues and the efforts that must be made to embrace a new type of contract with workers.

As seen in Figure 6.3, only about one in four workers is truly loyal, meaning they want to stay with their organization and they indeed plan to stay for at least two years. These workers not only feel good about where they are and know where they fit in, they're not actively looking at other opportunities. Typically high performers, they are willing to go the extra mile to get the job done and often act as role models for their peers. Across industries, workers in wholesale trade and financial services showed the highest levels of true loyalty, with 31 percent of the respondents from these industries in that category.

There were fewer than expected accessible employees (just 4 percent). These are the people who feel good about where they are and are positive about their organization, but they are not planning to stay with the organization for the next two years. These may be people looking for a career change or changing for situational reasons. The lack of numbers here indicates the strong impact that attitude or satisfaction has on people's retention.

A large chunk of the remaining workers in the United States falls into the trapped category: 39 percent. These people don't necessarily want to stay with their existing employer, but for one reason or another plan to stay put for the time being. The highest percentage of trapped employees among major sectors is found in public adminis-

Truly Loyal: 24%	Accessible: 4%	Trapped: 39%	High Risk: 33%
Want to stay	*May not stay*	*Don't want to stay but have to stay*	*Don't need to or want to stay*

FIGURE 6.3   Respondents to the 1999 Survey

tration/government (49 percent). Many government employees can look ahead to attractive pension/retirement plans and may feel they lack viable career options outside of government.

Having trapped workers probably challenges management with motivation and productivity issues with these employees. The survey data prove that being there is not the same as being excited about being there. Another unpleasant reality is that some of the trapped must include the lesser performers (less employable elsewhere) who are either less able or willing to go beyond the call of duty to achieve the objectives of the organization.

The last group, the high risk employees, contains an alarmingly high incidence of U.S. workers: 33 percent of all workers in this study. These employees not only don't want to be with their organization, they don't intend to stay there for the next two years. They have checked out emotionally and plan to "vote with their feet" in the near term. For the time that they do stay with the organization they may be more likely to behave as trapped employees, in terms of sub-optimal productivity and possibly negative word-of-mouth perceptions of their organization. When online, these are often the employees who check Monster.com each day. The industries that had the greatest number of high risk employees included transportation (44 percent), business services (42 percent), retail trade (41 percent), and technology (41 percent).

One intriguing aspect of this study is its weighting of the factors that influence workers' commitment to their companies. Where employees divide 100 points among 11 factors, five emerged as the ones that carried the most weight in the overall analysis. Listed in rank order from the highest influencer, they include:

1. Fairness at work—belief that the company treats them fairly and equitably, including rules and policies, and perceptions of fair pay.
2. Concern for employees—belief that the company shows care and concern, provides family-friendly benefits, and has managers/supervisors paying attention to the people who report to them.
3. Satisfaction with day-to-day work—feelings about the typical duties and activities, opportunities to grow and develop, and the amount of responsibility entrusted to them.
4. Trust in employees—feeling trusted to do their jobs in line with the organizational goals and being encouraged to try new approaches at work.
5. Reputation of the organization—admiring their companies, seeing them as being reputable and creditable in the marketplace, and believing in strategies, activities, and programs their organizations undertake.

Organizations were generally weaker in the area of care and concern for employees. High risk employees gave notably high negatives to their employers for not developing people for the long term and to management for not paying enough attention to people.

Fairness at work poses another challenge. Here, the high negatives among the high risk employees were in unfair compensation or pay and in not having policies carried out very fairly. Leaders must consider how to improve retention and attraction of the right employees to their organizations. Competitive pay and policies are more foundational or serve as minimal requirements, while the deciding factors in rebuilding relationships are the softer areas such as investing in continuous skill development, ensuring that policies and practices are applied equitably, and creating a culture in which people feel that they are paid attention to by various levels of management and associates.[27]

Employee Commitment Assessment Systems

James Kelly of UPS certainly made it clear that getting feedback from employees should be a significant performance metric for any corporation. In becoming more metric-managed, many companies have struggled particularly with the issue of meaningful employee feedback. A study reported in the March 1996 issue of *Management Review* showed many large companies using employee surveys and other feedback mechanisms, but leaders did not trust the quality of the information or know how to use it properly. Figure 6.4 indicates that although two out of three large firms were tracking information related to employee feedback and performance, only one out of six considered the information to be highly reliable. This contrasted with 61 percent who believed their financial information was reliable.[28]

> ### Sample "Killer" Employee Survey Indicators:
>
> Do the employees intend to stay in the organization at least the next two years?
> Would they recommend your organization to others as a good place to work?
> Do they feel your leadership and policies reflect care and concern for the employees?

As somebody once said, "Nobody wants to really ask employees what they want, because it's too hard to figure out exactly how to give them what they want." Leaders must be bold and insist that they get valid measures of employee commitment. There has never been a greater need to understand employees and their point of view. We recommend the efficient use of employee surveys to gather evaluations that can be built into a model of loyalty for employees. Business leaders rise to the challenge of finding out what employees want because the information itself can be a catalyst for making necessary changes to retain the people we need to keep.

Part of the reason for mistrusting employee feedback has been that the wrong questions have been asked—those that focus only on feelings about the corporate culture or on assessing benefits and pay rather

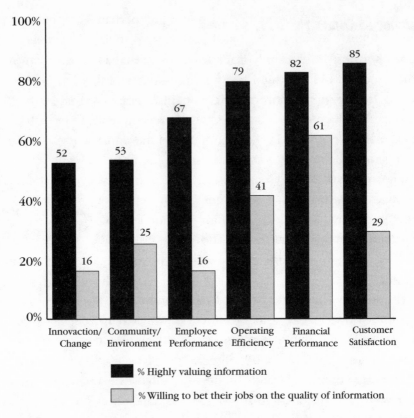

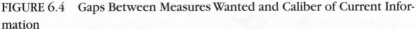

FIGURE 6.4   Gaps Between Measures Wanted and Caliber of Current Information

Source: J. Lingle and W. Schiemann "From Balanced Scorecard to Strategic Gauges: Is Measurement Worth It?" *Management Review* (March 1996): 56–61.

than the more bottom-line concern of retaining committed employees. From our work in this area, we recommend that employee survey programs include proven indicators of employee commitment, along with other pertinent questions (see the sidebar on the previoius page).

Another reason for mistrust is, in the immortal words of Jack Nicholson as Colonel Jessup in the 1992 film *A Few Good Men:* "You want the truth? You can't handle the truth!" Joe Folkman, author of *Employee Surveys That Make a Difference,* writes, "Objective information that contradicts our (organization's) self image is incredibly powerful."[29] In other words, business leaders don't always want to know the truth—

they can virtually count on being surprised and perhaps disappointed when reading feedback from employees regarding their perceptions of leadership, values, organizational practices, job satisfaction, and so forth. But once we move beyond questioning the validity of the data, we begin accepting that employees think differently than we thought they did. That realization in turn forces good managers to change their own assumptions and create initiatives to address the unmet needs of the employees. Sometimes an unmet need turns out to be a miscommunication or a lack of clarification of what leadership is really trying to accomplish. At that point you at least know that steps should be taken to rectify the misunderstanding, hopefully in a nondefensive way.

Some of the common reasons that leading organizations systematically use employee surveys are

- as a reality check and a catalyst for change;
- to measure progress in specific initiatives and programs undertaken to support employee loyalty and retention and attitudes;
- to assess risks to productivity, or from employee defections based on their attitudes and intentions; and
- to assess the needs of different locations, functional teams, and business units of the company relative to allocating resources for learning and development.

If the new contract with employees requires us to integrate their jobs with corporate strategy and give them a greater voice in the company while expecting more independence and responsibility on their part, then good surveys can help. Providing employees with a chance to assess thoroughly the organization and their relationship with it will address their need to be more engaged.

On the other hand, the company must then be visible in following up on employee findings. Managers at all levels should review the key findings and launch appropriate new initiatives or remedial actions— and communicate this information to employees. Employees feel exploited without seeing management take action on the results of the survey, possibly making the situation worse than not doing the study in the first place.

Relationship-assessing surveys should be taken at least annually so there can be in-process updates of progress and initiatives. Employee surveys have become easier to administer within organizations where most people have access to the Internet and e-mail. Even without technology, the surveys can be inexpensively administered by mailing questionnaires to people's homes or distributing them through internal mail. Confidentiality must be maintained throughout the process to ensure open and honest answers as well as high levels of cooperation.

Some of the most valuable information coming back from employee survey analysis includes the breakdowns by the different parts of your organization. This information allows communications and support programs to zero in on where the resources are the most needed. Reports should also direct the information to use as one of your performance metrics and provide in-depth reporting of the important opportunities needing attention at a corporate level, as well as by major business units or functional teams. In addition, important strengths that can be leveraged should be noted and communicated within and perhaps outside the company, citing any model teams or business units whose practices can be emulated.

A crucial facet of any employee survey work is the follow-up phase, when managers further probe particular problems or issues that were raised during the survey. By adding this additional wave of feedback, the specific initiatives needing to be undertaken and the particular problems to be solved in a given district or location become clearer. Leading people effectively in large organizations will mean establishing specific goals regarding relationships with employees—and using measures that track progress toward those goals.

Gates of Employee Loyalty:
Guidelines to Goals and Measures

The rule of thumb on goals and measures, of course, is that you have to have the right ones. The Gates of Employee Loyalty provide a check on the types of people goals and measures that leading organizations should have in place in the twenty-first century.

Gate One: Awareness for Current and Prospective Employees

If your company doesn't have an interactive website with links for applicants, you're already behind. As workers increasingly manage their own careers, they expect information regarding your firm to be available in a variety of places, including the recruiting sites, with links from your home website. Also, the appearance of your home site will send an impression of your firm, including its technological capabilities. Awareness has long been a function of the type of reputation your firm has at a corporate level. Much has to do with the effective managing of communications about your company, but otherwise, it's a longer-term result of good business practices, employee satisfaction, and word-of-mouth by your existing employees.

Your business can develop key metrics from the volume of people making inquiries about your company either at the website or through other means. There could be tracking of the number of applicants, number of offers and percent of offers accepted, and so forth.

Gate Two: Employee Knowledge

These measures begin with tracking the effectiveness of your communications inside the organization. Beyond the use of communication channels, surveys should reflect the degree to which employees are being equipped and supported in their jobs. This information relates specifically to the caliber of ongoing training and knowledge sharing throughout the organization. Last but not least would be feedback on how well employees understand and embrace the core values and ethics of the organization.

Gate Three: Admiration

It's worth saying again that in setting employee goals for Admiration, the operative word is *trust*. In a recent survey by Watson Wyatt Worldwide, one of the top drivers of employee commitment was "trust in senior leadership." Interestingly, the other key driver of employee commitment from the same study was the "chance to use (one's) skills."[30] This information seems to mirror what had been observed and was being taught by James Kelly at UPS: that employees must be given a greater stake and be more effectively engaged in carrying out the company's vision by having the "toolbox" of support and skills to help them make a contribution. *CFO Magazine* quoted the vice president of human resources at Yahoo, Inc., Kurk Froggatt, who claims that employees are really driven by an "emotional commitment: Do I feel valued, challenged, and capable of making a difference? And is the day-to-day experience energizing? Because if it isn't, I don't have to stay here."[31] Chris Carlton, a human resources executive from Network Appliance, Inc., a Sunnyvale, California, network data storage maker, says that when employees leave it's because "We haven't paid attention to them. They didn't feel valued from an ongoing stock perspective or from a work environment perspective."[32] The measures for Admiration must come from the voice of the employee, and we must seek out and heed them before they reach us from exit interviews.

Gate Four: Employee Actions

Much of what we are talking about can be known from the simple measurement of employee loyalty and the elements that drive it. Other indicators would be any measure of employees making positive referrals to recruit other prospective employees to the organization. The willingness of employees to volunteer in areas of corporate responsibility or outreach, such as United Way programs, or to act as role models or mentors for their peers or for new workers, is an important sign of the kind of action that leaders hope to see evolve from strong feelings of commitment to the organization.

. . . .

Case in Point: Stalcop and Employee Relationship Assessment

In 1997, Ron St. Clair, President of Stalcop, an international manufacturer of components for electrical, automotive original equipment and replacement parts, faced a situation of stagnant growth for the firm and a tightening labor market as well. Competition in these markets had intensified over the years since Stalcop was founded in 1981 by individuals with unique experience in the copper cold-forming process. The firm, still headquartered in Thorntown, Indiana, was sold to 131 Capital Corp. in 1993, investing Stalcop with funds to expand the business. Today, in addition to its emphasis on making copper components, the company offers plastic injection-molded parts for the healthcare, computer, automotive, and other industries. It is an international firm, with the plastics business based in Ireland and another specialty manufacturer based in Germany.

The word *Stalcop* is an acronym derived by its founders from *St*eel, *Al*uminum, and *Cop*per, the metals applicable to the cold-forming process. Despite its expertise in the cold-forming process and a reputation for product quality and customer service, Stalcop's competitors were by the mid-1990s matching them in price, quality, and delivery. "The normal differentiators were (now) commodities," says St. Clair.[33] There was additionally some mistrust of management by employees stemming from the transition to new ownership in 1993. Some policy changes had been made, the kind that go hand-in-hand with transitioning from an entrepreneurial firm to one that is professionally managed. (As one example in Stalcop's case, the new management no longer allowed the employees in the small-town–based firm to charge groceries from the local store to Stalcop, which would be billed by the store and then reimbursed by the employees.) Management openly presented a rationale for such changes at the time they were made.[34]

In 1997, top management made a key strategic decision: "We needed to make customer satisfaction and employee commitment the new differentiators for Stalcop," says St. Clair.[35] In sizing up their business situation, St. Clair and his staff felt they simply must figure out how to become more effective in their relationships with customers and employees as well. They viewed these as strategic necessities. Also believing in measurement of strategic priorities, the company planned to take semi-annual relationship assessments from employees as well as customers over at least a five-year period. This methodology would track the impact of making changes in policies, operations, and communications to fulfill the company's new strategy with associates and customers. What management didn't know was the degree to which the new business metric approach and the new strategy were destined to permanently alter Stalcop's corporate culture.

The program began by surveying employees, realizing that more highly committed personnel would better carry out new means to strengthen customer satisfaction. The story of the program and its impact to date may be best told by highlighting the events from the point of beginning the employee assessment program.

The Events

- June 1998: Questionnaires are distributed and, with help from the consulting firm, Stalcop executives receive their baseline report on employee commitment showing trust, fairness, and concern for employees to be "hot" relationship issues—areas that employees want the company to improve on and which, they also say, are key influencers or drivers of their overall commitment. Management was somewhat surprised and disappointed because they felt they had diligently communicated the rationale for needed organizational changes, but the survey showed these messages either had not been believed or had not been understood.
- August 1998: Stalcop forms a peer-nominated employee group to act on findings.
- September 1998: The Associate Advisory Group (AAG) creates the "I have a question" program. All employees may ask any question of management with the guarantee of a published answer and anonymity.

- November 1998: Leadership team is to be held responsible for improving employee scores.
- January 1999: Linking "I have a question" comments to survey data reveals employees don't feel they can readily purchase the tools they need to do their daily work, such as machine upkeep.
- February 1999: A new tool-ordering process for employees is created, giving easier access to get approval for new items and to find out the status of those orders.
- June 1999: Stalcop creates a company-wide mentor program to help new hires learn policies, procedures, and operating skills. Successful integration means a mentor receives a cash bonus 90 and 180 days after the new employee's start date.

The Outcomes

By late 1999 (or within 18 months of the baseline analysis of employee feedback), employees' positive ratings of Stalcop were on the rise. "They felt more listened to": up 27 percentage points. "They had their ideas better put into practice": up 21 points. Perceptions of receiving fair treatment and of management showing genuine care and concern had risen by 18 points. And the mentoring program had driven the positive ratings of "Stalcop provides enough training and development to help me do my work" up 24 percentage points.

To sum it up, employees were feeling very good about their company. St. Clair related that, "instead of new workers being shunned, they have people (their assigned mentors) interested in seeing them succeed. And we have mentors pretty excited about this as well."[36] Perceptions of Stalcop's products and services had risen by 16 percentage points, and feelings that the company was well run saw a 23 percent increase. One of the largest gains in feelings of commitment to Stalcop was the 29-point increase in response to the statement that they "feel part of the family at Stalcop." According to St. Clair, who well remembers the generally glum, uncooperative atmosphere before the surveys, "we now have much more of a core group who want to be here and they have become less forgiving of those (few) who still don't."[37]

Addressing employee work issues directly and promptly had enhanced employees' commitment to Stalcop, as well as their motivation to do excellent work. Stalcop's increasingly dedicated workforce carried out initiatives to address customer issues, which led to a 32-point increase in excellent/very good ratings by customers of customer service. Comparison to the competition in customer surveys today shows Stalcop now outscores them on 59 of 63 benchmarks.[38]

Doug Grisaffe, Chief Methodologist for Walker Information, has spent time analyzing the Stalcop employee and customer data for a paper currently under review for publication in the *Journal of Customer Satisfaction/Dissatisfaction and Complaining Behavior.* He has observed an important correlation between employee and customer commitment improvements and, in turn, a distinct relationship between improved customer scores and top-line financial performance (sales per account were up over time in accordance with higher loyalty ratings by customers). As Grisaffe puts it, "An interconnected system appears to be in place where simultaneous employee and customer measurements led to targeted improvement actions that ultimately related to (more) sales."[39] From the data and discussions with Stalcop, he concludes that solving the workplace issues enhanced employee motivation, which, combined with initiatives addressing customer issues, led to greater customer loyalty and repurchasing.

Many companies today are hesitant even to ask employees for feedback, either because they don't want to see the results or because they don't want to address the perceptions and issues that would be revealed. For that reason, the executives and owners of Stalcop should be recognized not only for investing in the feedback loop, but for making sure that the results created initiatives and a different company than before. CEO Ron St. Clair in particular has invested a great deal of personal effort in using this system. As he said about this attention to measuring stakeholder perceptions, "My staff thinks I don't have time to do this. I don't have time not to." Hard work to unleash the power of the associates at Stalcop has definitely paid off, both in greater goodwill internally, with customers and in the company's performance.[40]

....

From One Stakeholder to Another. . .

Stalcop has exemplified leading by knowing the truth about customer and employee perceptions. This case also introduces a new principle: that enhancing relationships with our internal constituents—employees—will logically help organizations build up their relationships with customers. Much more is said about this linkage and other stakeholder relationships in Chapter 9.

In Chapter 7 we consider those other outside constituencies beyond customers that virtually any organization must maintain good personal relationships with to be successful in the long term. These range from community leaders or media, who may have a great deal to say about our corporate reputations, to contacts within the capital markets (investors), to trade associations, and even to competitors. One special constituency addressed is our vendors or alliance partners, because companies increasingly rely on such partnerships. All these outside groups make up what we call "extended stakeholders."

The Power of Extended Stakeholders

ccording to Monster.com and the *Wall Street Journal*, "94% of successful job seekers claimed that networking had made all the difference for them."[1] We instinctively go beyond the inner circle of close friends and family when we need to learn new things, ask for help or special expertise, and make others aware of who we are. And businesses and other organizations do so as well. Businesses must go beyond the inner circle of owners, employees, and customers to establish viable relationships with other people and organizations. These other relationships might lead to additional sources of sales and revenue and new ways to distribute products and services. The contacts are also the means to maintaining a positive reputation and goodwill.

One way to distinguish these outside business relationships from those we have already discussed is an analogy with our family structures in society. Many cultures categorize the relatives we live with as our *immediate* family, typically our spouse, parents, children, and siblings. The *extended* family may include grandparents, uncles, aunts, and cousins. Similar language can be used to describe categories of stakeholders. Customers, employees, and owners or investors would be considered the *immediate,* or *core,* stakeholders, because these are the ones we "live with" every day. But as in our families, we have close relations with and obligations to the rest of the family as well—the *extended* stakeholders of the business.

All in the Family

Who makes up the extended "family" of stakeholders? Table 7.1 contains a fairly comprehensive list. Remember that stakeholders are defined as people who have some stake in your organization while your organization, in turn, has a stake in them. Certain constituencies are more important or relevant to some business categories than others or are more integral to an individual business strategy. But it's fair to say that in addition to customers, employees, and investors, every organization has extended stakeholder groups with whom they should be very actively engaged.

Walker Information's 1999 international study of business executives confirmed that businesses do recognize extended constituents. Although the study didn't probe as comprehensive a list of possible stakeholders as shown in Table 7.1, it found that a majority of business leaders think of suppliers, the community, and the government as being their stakeholders, and nearly half place financial analysts in that category as well. It was less certain whether the typical business leader makes these constituencies a high priority for effectively building and maintaining relationships. Figure 7.1 shows the various stakeholder groups recognized by most executives.

One indication of whether a stakeholder group is a business priority is if the group is mentioned in the mission statement and values of the corporation. Executives around the world state the importance of immediate stakeholders to their business in their corporate mission statements or core values: customers (82 percent), employees (70

TABLE 7.1   Immediate and Extended Stakeholders

Immediate Stakeholders	Extended Stakeholders
Individual investors	Unions
Institutional investors	Suppliers
Customers	Alliance partners
Employees	Industry associations
	Local communities
	Consumer/user associations
	Special interest groups/NGOs
	Media
	Government regulators
	Competitors
	Outside board directors
	The general public (beyond local communities)
	Financial analysts
	Lenders
	Education leaders

percent), and shareholders (57 percent). But the extended stakeholders are mentioned with far less frequency (see Figure 7.2).[2]

We have made the case that business leaders' fixation with shareholder value and the migration to so many new ways of doing business have undermined the commitment of the immediate stakeholders. Customers are now on the lookout for the best value they can find and want to use whichever model or technology fits their preferences and life/work styles. Employees have been "mugged-by-reality" to have more loyalty for their personal skills development and career than for the organization they work in. Spurred on by the advent of online transactions and a fluctuating market, we now have day-traders and a tendency toward IPOs and short-term stock investments as investors attempt to catch the next growing company's wave at just the right time.

If immediate stakeholders' loyalties to corporations have decreased, then we can also assume that the sense of loyalty has dwindled for the extended constituents who are typically less of a priority

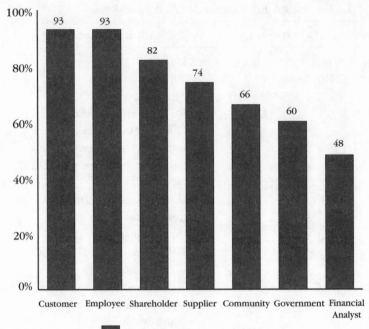

Overall % to Name as Stakeholder

FIGURE 7.1   How Stakeholders Stack Up Around the World
   Source:Walker Information and Hudson Institute, sponsors,"1999 national
Business Ethics Study," www.walkerinfo.com.

to management to begin with. In some cases, extended stakeholders
are skeptical of businesses because it's their job to be. Unions and
consumer activist groups are adversaries to corporations almost by
definition (which is not to say that a mutually beneficial collaboration
can't be developed). Government regulators and legislators, NGOs,
and even the media generally see themselves as being watchdogs
over commercial enterprises. The general public and local communities, influenced as they have been by film and media and, at times,
personal experience, may be inclined to question the honesty and
fairness of business practices in general.

So giving extended stakeholders mention in corporate mission
statements and in core values is a great first step. But business leaders
must then proceed beyond lip service and build relationships with

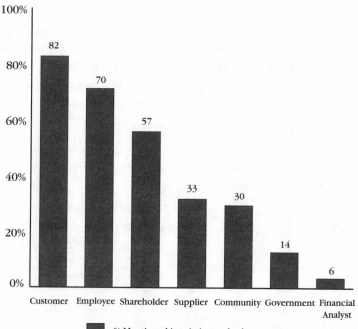

FIGURE 7.2   Extent to Which Companies Include Stakeholders in Mission/Value Statements

Source: Walker Information and Hudson Institute, sponsors, "1999 National Business Ethics Study," www.walkerinfo.com.

the extended stakeholders who are important to their business or to whom the company has made a commitment. This process will require a plan to reach out to constituents and move them through the gates of loyalty, from awareness of your firm through knowledge, to admiration, and ultimately to the desired actions and recommendations that support your corporate goals.

Different Folks for Different Strokes

Reaching out to collaborate better with constituents such as media, community leaders, and legislators definitely requires an investment of resources, so it is important to size up the relative importance of our relationships with these various groups. A good way to set priorities is to profile individually the extended stakeholder segments with whom you should potentially collaborate and then ask the following questions of your executive and corporate communications staff and your public relations leaders/consultants (who are most likely to have the best knowledge of multiple extended stakeholder segments):

- How much of a stake do we have in the goodwill and support of people in this group? How have they helped us or others like us in the past? In what other ways could they possibly help?
- What risks do we incur if unexpected events would lead to a withdrawal of support by or even antagonism from this group? Have we ever lost their support in the past? In what ways could we be at risk with this group?
- What commitments have we already made to this group that it would be unethical not to keep? What new commitments should be made that would be in line with our mission and strategy?

At the end of such a discussion, there should be enough input to use team voting or scoring techniques to assign relative scores to each extended stakeholder to help determine the segments requiring new or continued attention and resources. Those choices will clearly differ by business category, as illustrated in the examples of crucial relationships selected by members of these sectors (see Table 7.2).

Co-Evolving with Suppliers

One extended stakeholder group that has experienced an evolving relationship with its customers in the past several years is suppliers. Companies have worked overtime to prune one business after another from the family tree to focus energy on core operations and competencies and reduce costs. They have worked tirelessly to smooth every possible bottleneck in the supply chain, speeding the flow of innovation, goods, and services to the marketplace. These two

TABLE 7.2   Crucial Relationships by Business Category

Manfacturing	**Construction Contractors**
Suppliers/alliance partners	Suppliers
Communities near facilities	Local officials
State/federal regulations	Environmental action groups

Pharmaceuticals	**Industry Associations**
Regulators	Media
Media	Regulators
Managed care organizations	Industry opinion leaders

trends have dramatically affected suppliers and their relationships with their clients at the same time that they increasingly have created value for end-user customers. The trend also spotlights a new corporate imperative: to rebuild supplier relationships and commitment.

The supplier story relates in some degree to firms that in recent years have been called "category killers": businesses such as Amazon.com, which come up with new models for doing business, enabling tremendous growth and eventually dominating long-existing business categories. They not only kill off competitors, they permanently change the way business is done in those industries. Retail category killers include Wal-Mart in the discount trade, Home Depot in hardware, and Staples in office supplies. These firms achieved success by casting whole new business designs that made breakthroughs in the amount of value delivered to customers. Beyond the category killers, certain manufacturing sectors have transformed processes and entire distribution channels in response to global competition. Their initiatives usually put them ahead of competitors by one or more years. And often at the very heart of virtually all of these new concepts is a new vision for the supply chain.

James F. Moore, international advisor on business strategy, described this concept in *The Harvard Business Review* and in his 1995 bestseller, *The Death of Competition*. He used biological systems as a metaphor, since the visionary business leaders in a sense are creating new "ecosystems" for their businesses. Armed with their unique understanding of bypassing the traditional multi-division organization and instead building a more flexible system from the ground up using the most powerful information systems and new technology available, these leaders collaborate with other organizations to establish new chains of supply that ultimately enhance value to customers.[3]

Businesses historically have sought success with an approach that is like winning a game: You must simply beat the other players (competitors). But the approach described by Moore isn't just squaring off with competitors—it is like changing all the rules to be in your favor (without cheating!). He quotes Bill Joy of Sun Microsystems: "The goal is not to win at someone else's game, but rather to change the game to one that you can win."[4]

The auto industry provides one example of changing the rules. Major companies such as Ford and Chrysler are no longer just trying to go head-to-head. Instead, they are creating entire new communities that link suppliers and strategic alliance partners to each other and ultimately to customers, all with the intent of maximizing customer value.

Japan, of course, led the way in creating this new "game," although U.S. manufacturers continue finding ways to adapt and improve upon it. Following devastation in World War II, Japanese business leaders realized that they had to develop a very different model of business. Unlike their U.S. counterparts, they were forced to optimize their resources and were open to suggestions from W. Edwards Deming, Joseph Juran, and others in the movement that became the total quality management revolution.

This willingness to think and work differently led to the creation of new sophisticated systems deploying customer needs carefully into design aspects, using techniques of concurrent R&D and engineering, empowering workers, and linking together networks of suppliers using management practices of statistical sophistication. The outcome was similar to that in the Xerox case cited previously: a product of enormous value in terms of features, variety, and product quality for the price.

The "Lambs" Stay Alert

Wal-Mart is another well-known case of reinventing the game, complete with its visionary creation of a complex web of supply, unheard-of economies of scale, and considerable leverage in their supplier relationships. The devastating impact upon its competitors (K-Mart and the legions of small-town retailers) has become a business legend. But in thinking not only of Wal-Mart but of all the revolutionized categories, what has been the impact on the suppliers throughout this process? And what needs to be done in building and maintaining relationships with them today? In the auto industry as well as in other industrial segments, many suppliers would agree that at least early in the process, suppliers were being exploited by being asked to hold more inventory and to deliver it just-in-time or cut prices.

I remember an old Woody Allen joke that describes the new "partnerships" between customers and suppliers: "The lion will lay down with the lamb . . . but the lamb gets no sleep!" Suppliers had reason to be wary when the manufacturers returned from Japan describing new "partnerships," because the new partnerships often amounted to a more intense scrutiny of their practices, lower prices, and larger inventory.

The predicament of suppliers in the auto industry at the time has been described by Allan Kennedy, management consultant and author of *The End of Shareholder Value*. Suppliers absorbed the impact of just-in-time inventory practices by making smaller and more frequent shipments of components to the assembler. Inventory came off the balance sheet of the major manufacturers and back onto the books of the suppliers. Suppliers were forced to adopt practices learned from the Japanese before the manufacturers figured them out for their own operations.[5]

The other major change for suppliers was increased bidding pressures for lower prices (and margins). The auto industry and sectors have gone to a first-tier supply system, where a shorter list of suppliers is approved or preferred. This narrower span of relationships allows the manufacturer to outsource more work and exercise greater control.

Making the first-tier list of suppliers meant receiving more attention from the manufacturer in terms of quality ratings, productivity evaluations, and of course, cost assessments. In return, the suppliers received longer-term contracts. But this assurance of future business is a double-edged sword: The suppliers are locked into prices, and margins then erode if costs go up faster than anticipated. Smaller firms, of course, suffered the most under the conditions described here. Many suppliers were sold or went out of business because manufacturers reduced supplier lists and required higher standards.

Kennedy describes how suppliers have responded by "striking back" against the conditions that manufacturers have imposed on them. The major tactic has been the proliferation of mergers and acquisitions among suppliers. "Of the approximately 5,000 U.S. automotive supply companies in existence in 1990, almost half of them had disappeared by 1999," he noted.[6] In one extreme example, Lear Corp. and Johnson Controls now control almost 80 percent of the car seat market in the United States, and in Europe they share the market with just one other supplier.

Through acquisition, certain suppliers have expanded their positions considerably, with the aspiration to become major players in the new "ecosystem" actually created by the major manufacturers. Kennedy has observed this trend transpiring not just in the auto industry, but in office equipment, telecommunications, computers, retailing, and airplane manufacturing. And, he predicts, "If any of these consolidating industries want a peek at the future, they might just well look at the computer industry and notice what clout Microsoft and Intel exercise even though their main products are components of the final product shipped to consumers."[7]

So there has clearly developed a tug-of-war between manufacturers and their suppliers, with the advantage seesawing over time. This co-evolution would ideally have been achieved with greater collaboration between the assemblers and their suppliers rather than with each party mainly seeking its own self-interest and then having to respond later to unpleasant new realities created by the other party.

One approach in trying to establish a better-networked supply system is to have more interactive, face-to-face encounters with suppliers, working toward mutual goals. This approach begins by developing a corporate value for real partnerships that seek joint benefits. It also would mean arranging periodic and thorough assessments of the relationship from the supplier perspective as well as ongoing feedback regarding one's own strategies. The following case study is an example of an organization that has invested in such an effort.

••

Case in Point: The Shiel Sexton Company

Shiel Sexton of Indianapolis was started in 1962 by two partners who shared a philosophy of providing construction services as a merit shop contractor. In construction, "merit" shop means the company competes based on the merit or value offered to customers, in terms of meeting industry safety and quality standards, with construction done on time and on budget. This philosophy embodies open competitive bidding on jobs and compliance with the legal boundaries of employee compensation, safety, and nondiscrimination. Merit firms bid predominantly, but not exclusively, on projects allowing nonunion craft people.

Shiel Sexton has developed its expertise in commercial, industrial, and retail construction, becoming one of the largest providers of construction services in Indianapolis, with 220 employees and over $150 million in annual revenue. Given the sheer variety of skilled work involved in different phases of their construction projects, Shiel Sexton also typifies an industry that must mesh together a virtual web of suppliers even to function.

Shiel Sexton has worked to develop strong relationships with its subcontractors and suppliers—architectural, electrical, masonry, plumbing, roofing, carpentry, landscaping, pipe fitting, and welding worker make up just a partial list. Andy Shiel, chief executive of the company, is open about the firm's reliance on these relationships. The associates of subcontracting firms help craft the quality of the end product, sometimes interact with customers more directly, and are an important part of the value chain, just as are direct employees.

As the company grew in size, the reliance on suppliers and the ongoing challenge of staffing new projects grew as well. Shiel Sexton management came to believe they could be more competitive in winning bids and in demanding quality work by earning an even stronger commitment from the subcontractor firms. In 1999, Shiel engaged with a consultant to interview nearly 1,000 subcontractors across all of the crafts that they hire. The purpose was to assess the working relationships with the subcontractors and Shiel Sexton's reputation as a contractor and then prioritize issues that were most important or could be improved to enhance supplier commitment.

The structured questionnaire obtained ratings of Shiel Sexton relative to other contractors on items in such areas as

- the regular use (hiring) of the subcontractor;
- the field supervisor's management skills and fairness;
- fairness in accounting/payment practices; and
- the general reputation of Shiel Sexton.

The survey analysis determined a clearer path toward commitment by the subcontracting firms, as indicated by their willingness to continue selling their services to the contractor and to say positive things about it to others in the industry. Shiel Sexton held a number of internal meetings to discuss the findings and their implications. Scrutiny was given to the answers given by individual suppliers, and any lingering issues were handled by the individual most responsible for those relationships.

The broader issues were considered as well. As one example, many subcontractors wanted to be paid more quickly after their part of the project was finished. This prompted Shiel Sexton management to revise its company policies and adjust procedures to make more timely payments.

After considering the suppliers' concerns about always having the right tools at job sites, Shiel started a business for renting on site to subcontractors the scaffolding, space heaters, and other equipment required in their work. This freed the suppliers from the costs and hassles of hauling the stuff around themselves. The new rental program also cut supplier costs and further boosted commitment, while also, of course, giving Shiel Sexton a new source of revenue.

Making an investment such as Shiel Sexton's in understanding the expectations of suppliers strikes a refreshing balance in the dynamics of corporate-vendor relationships. Most firms want to walk the line of demanding productivity, quality, and flexibility from suppliers while at the same time working to support their loyal, effective vendors. Taking the Shiel Sexton approach would help us remember the second part of that balanced goal: to understand and support them in ways that earn supplier commitment.

....

Where Everybody Knows Your Name: Corporate Reputation

Certain extended stakeholders have face-to-face encounters with a company in the course of a relationship: with suppliers in the working relationship, with government regulators who have oversight and arrange periodic meetings, and even with financial analysts most closely following leading firms in their sector. But many of the remaining extended stakeholders may not even be aware of your company and its values unless you inform them. For such groups we must communicate the values and facts about our companies if we want to become better known and supported by them. And it is equally important to be aware of the risk of unexpected crises as well as to be prepared to manage outside communications when a disaster hits, learning the art of being straight with the facts while presenting your side of the issue at hand.

A company's ethics or character is defined in the minds of stakeholders not only by how it performs but also by how it lives out the values it holds. Actions become the reputation of a company, the perception that others have of it. And corporate reputation in today's realm of open communications and instant news has never been more critical.

We define *corporate reputation* as the reflection of an organization over time as seen through the eyes of its stakeholders and expressed through their thoughts and words. Think about what shapes our view of a person or an organization: It either comes through what we've seen or experienced firsthand or from what we have heard or read about the entity. From that view, we form an expectation of how someone might behave in the future. It's a "reflection" rather than the whole truth about people or companies, but that reflection or perception becomes the reality in terms of how people behave toward them.

Is Corporate Reputation the Same as Brand Equity?

The concept of *brand equity* is based on the idea that consumers will pay more for the quality and value they associate with products and services carrying a certain name. As such, brand equity is a narrower construct than *reputation,* because it's about the support from and interactions with a single stakeholder group, consumers or buyers. *Corporate reputation* is about the interactions with multiple stakeholder groups.

In measuring corporate reputation, we would normally examine aspects of business activities and performance beyond just products and services. However, the assessment would include a short battery of attributes designed to measure the importance of brand equity in the reputation equation. We discuss in greater detail later in this chapter the breadth of issues needing to be evaluated for a full measure of corporate reputation.

More than Corporate Image

Another common question is whether corporate reputation is simply image. These two are more entwined, but reputation is actually more than image. *Image* comes about from the portrayal of a company's features and values to those who are not directly encountering the company, such as opinion leaders we may not know or the general public that uses consumer products but never actually speaks with the manufacturer, only to the retailer or reseller. But reputation more broadly represents the views of all stakeholders, those having direct experience, such as customers and employees, as well as those who must rely solely on their image of the firm.

Handling corporate image is the stuff of investor relations, packaging designs, advertising, public relations, and what our politicians have now exemplified as "spin." Creating and maintaining an image is certainly an important part of managing corporate reputation. We have to be certain that the image being communicated is grounded in reality and not just self-serving, because the truth seems always to come out in the end.

Pay Now or Pay Later

We have discussed in this book how tricky investing has become, because the stock-picker has to account less for the company's historical financial performance than for its upside prospects, emerging technical leadership, social responsibility, and other intangibles that simply do not exist on the balance sheet or in the performance criteria. Good management dictates that we now wrestle with identifying and measuring these assets that cannot be found in the financial statements. And it will be hard to find any that are more precious than corporate reputation.

To underscore the value of a reputation, consider what happens when a good company name gets lost or damaged by an incident that makes news. The cycle of business news-making has a premise that readers seek and media obligingly scour their leads to learn of trends and expected changes, but also mistakes, failures, scandals, ethical issues, and safety or ecological disasters. Some of these stories are unquestionably newsworthy. Some of them prove to have been very hard to avoid compared to other events. But you can be assured that when the company name hits the headlines, the total market value will take a hit, and it may take a long time to make it back to where it was.

We mentioned previously a very large study that indicated almost certain loss of market value on top of the direct costs following an issue viewed as being socially irresponsible. A study done by Charles Fombrun, author of *Reputation: Realizing Value from the Corporate Image,* compiled data from 12 corporate crises and found there was consistently about $1 billion in losses within a one-week window around the crisis.[8] It can take many years to replace a reputation once it is lost.

Yet crises occur with regularity, involving at times some of the largest and most impressive of the market leaders. Even the Disney name was recently associated with stealing the ideas of an entrepreneur. Probably the most prominent event at the time of this writing is the still-developing saga of Bridgestone/Firestone tire defects. One of the company's larger radial tires, which is standard equipment on Ford Explorers, is alleged to shred sometimes when driven at highway speeds, causing injuries and loss of life. The following headlines tell the tale, all reported on or around August 10, 2000; our brief comments have been added. At this point we can only speculate about the damage in dollars and cents to the reputation of the companies involved:[9]

- "Bridgestone/Firestone Set to Replace 6.5 Million Tires" (the second-largest tire recall in history)
- "Bridgestone Cuts Profit Forecast After U.S. Unit Issues Tire Recall" (This probably accounts for the cost of recall; total costs, including legal costs and market value, are yet to be tallied.)
- "Auto Safety Group Files Suit to Pressure Ford, Firestone to Expand Tire Recall" (Here come the NGOs and activist stakeholders, not to mention the start of a possible avalanche in legal costs and subsequent announcements of legal actions.)
- "Firestone Tire Recall Could Mean Trouble Ahead for Market Share" (Some will undoubtedly be hesitant to buy/repurchase the Firestone brand [impact of reputation]. Competitors can be expected to leverage this problem, selling against the Firestone brand and possibly capturing market share in the process [reputation again].)

- "Senate to Hold Hearing About Firestone Recall" (Not all of us can claim having the U.S. Senate as a stakeholder. Of course, in this case that's like having *60 Minutes* as a stakeholder— neither desirable nor anticipated. *Lesson:* If you must have a crisis, avoid it during election years.)

The headline about loss in market share in this case supports earlier evidence that reputation influences buying and other forms of support from stakeholders. In 1994, Walker Information conducted a national study on corporate character and social responsibility that found that corporate reputation has a very strong impact on brand loyalty. In fact, 88 percent of consumers were more likely to buy from a company having a solid reputation. In addition, employees were more likely to work for such companies, and more than one in four investors said the business practices and ethics of firms were "extremely important" to their investment decisions.[10]

Reputation has been a key factor in choosing alliance partners and acquisition projects. Todd Saxton, professor of strategic management at Indiana University, conducted an exhaustive study of the link between reputation and performance of international alliances and acquisitions. The study analyzed approximately 570 alliances and acquisitions formed in 1993 in the chemicals, pharmaceuticals, and related industries. Through the three-year study, Saxton established a strong link between reputation and the success of these transactions. Specifically, product quality and management reputation had the greatest impact on alliance success, and product quality and financial reputation most affected acquisition success.[11]

In doing thorough survey assessments on all the dimensions of customer value and loyalty, we have noticed for years and across hundreds of studies that customer loyalty will often be driven as much by an image of their supplier as by competitive pricing or the quality of the product or service that they purchase. In other words, reputation adds value and helps drive loyalty—it can be as important as the other reasons that customers buy. The simple fact is that people— whether customers, employees, or other stakeholders—want to be associated with good companies. Conversely, they do not want to be associated with firms that have tainted reputations. Table 7.3 shows how reputation can affect the behavior of various constituents toward a business.

Prevention: The Preservative of Reputation

As one business reporter said, if we don't manage our own corporate reputations then someone else will. Our number one investment has to be in preventive maintenance: high standards of quality, safety, and environmental control that protect and assure our stakeholders.

The next level of reputation investment is being prepared for crises and having ongoing, professional communications with stakeholders, including media relations, investor relations, and regulatory relations. Proactive communications with stakeholders require managing relationships, but also asking for feedback and assessing reputation from the stakeholder perspective periodically.

Marketers have worked diligently to communicate to consumers the product traits and even corporate branding that differentiates them in the marketplace as well as to take a pulse on market acceptance. But only recently have executives shown interest in understanding and ultimately tracking corporate reputation. A recent survey of almost 600 chief executive officers and other senior managers released in February 2000 by global public relations firm Hill & Knowlton and *Chief Executive Magazine* reports that:[12]

- 96 percent of senior executives now believe that corporate reputation is very important.
- Over 90 percent believe that CEO visibility plays a key factor in building reputation.
- 65 percent say they dedicate more time to corporate reputation than they did five years ago.
- The percentage of companies actually measuring corporate reputation has doubled in one year. The incidence went from

TABLE 7.3 Effects of Reputation

Customers	Employee	Business Partners	Investors	Government and Media
• Amount they buy and price they pay • If they recommend or criticize • Resistance to competition • Latitude in crisis	• Talent level you attract and retain • Loyalty to the company • Commitment to company's success	• Favorable treatment • Level of commitment • Resistance to competition	• Stock price • Confidence and security levels in management's ability • Capital rates • Risk	• Favorable treatment • Latitude in crisis • Support on key initiatives

19 percent who formally measured corporate reputation in 1998 to 37 percent in the 1999 survey.

Study sponsor J. P. Donlan, Editor-in-Chief of *Chief Executive Magazine,* concludes that, "CEOs increasingly see reputation as an extension of their corporate brand—something to help sell goods and services, but also to be used as a recruiting tool. The wonder is that relatively few actually measure how they are doing."[13]

Measuring Corporate Reputation

Survey research techniques have been successfully applied to the problem of effectively measuring reputation. The essential principles are to include each stakeholder group (immediate as well as extended) whose collaboration can make a difference in maintaining the reputation you want. For example, a wholesaler or other business-to-business firm may not be as concerned about the general public's awareness and image of its firm as is a consumer goods/services firm. Consumer products firms, on the other hand, are rightfully concerned about public opinion. Although firms should be managing their reputations in the local communities where they reside, privately held firms wouldn't need the type of reputation assessment from financial analysts that a publicly traded one would.

The reason that managing reputation is important ties back to the notion of stakeholder commitment and loyalty. Members of local communities tell us whether they would support or otherwise speak well of the corporations located in their community or of corporate brands that they know well enough. This intention to support the firm (or not) rests largely on the image or reputation of the company. The effect of reputation on loyalty shows up in other stakeholders, such as the potential investors who care about the type of firms they invest in and potential employees who do their own investigations on the Web or network about prospective firms to learn what they are really like to work for.

No matter which stakeholders are assessing your firm, many of the same questions can be included in the surveys. Ratings on certain items contribute to the overall reputation of almost any firm. Many of these are shown in Figure 7.3 under the following headings:

Corporate Citizenship
Management Quality
Work Environment/Practices
Financial Performance
Market Leadership
Customer Focus
Product and Service Quality

Another principle of measuring reputation is to obtain ratings that compare your firm's reputation to that of other leading firms. There is almost no way to interpret people's ratings of your reputation except in relation to the view they have of other benchmark firms—ideally, firms in your category as well as ones that make the "most admired" type lists (not to say that those are mutually exclusive).

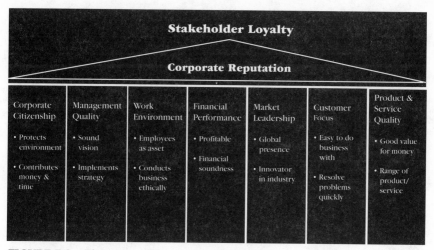

FIGURE 7.3   Elements of Corporate Reputation

Figure 7.4 shows the outcomes of the survey taken among an individual important segment, financial analysts. On each of the major dimensions, this client firm was compared by the financial analysts to each of two other leading corporations, ABC and XYZ. This summary grid highlights where the client firm turned out to be rated higher than one of the benchmark brands (designated "you"), where there was a statistical tie (designated by the symbol —), or where one of the benchmarks was rated higher than the client (designated by that benchmark company's name, either ABC or XYZ).

The results of a reputation survey should very naturally flow into making adjustments to company communications in general and targeting new public relations strategies that will improve certain stakeholder relationships in particular. Figure 7.5 indicates how the feedback might be presented to corporate teams, including executive staff and communications and public relations specialists. It reflects priorities to encourage decisions on new actions and project initiatives that will serve to bolster the reputation of the organization.

For example, the Top Priorities include all of the aspects of the perceived Market Leadership (or lack thereof): This firm was criticized in

| | **Who Outperforms:** | | | | | | | |
| | **Customer** | | **Financial** | | **Employees** | | **Community** | |
Benchmark Companies	**ABC**	**XYZ**	**ABC**	**XYZ**	**ABC**	**XYZ**	**ABC**	**XYZ**
Overall Reputation	You	XYZ	—	You	ABC	—	XYZ	—
Product/Service Quality	You	XYZ	You	You	You	You	—	You
Market Leadership	—	XYZ	ABC	—	ABC	XYZ	—	MNO
Customer	—	You	—	—	You	—	—	—
Managment Quality	You	XYZ	ABC	You	You	XYZ	—	MNO
Work Environment	—	XYZ	—	—	ABC	—	XYZ	—
Financial Performance	You	—	ABC	You	—	XYZ	—	You
Corporate Citizenship	—	XYZ	You	—	You	You	XYZ	You

FIGURE 7.4   Sample Results of Benchmarking Reputation Survey

the survey for not being the most innovative or dominant force in the industry. The managers should be considering better ways to emphasize to people the scope of their operations, their R&D investments, and their performance and growth to establish the Market Leadership reputation they at least deserve. The chart also reveals that they have some Leverageable Strengths in product/service quality (particularly attributes designated by C, E, and F codes). These specific perceptual strengths need to be further leveraged in communications with various segments.

Areas for Possible Improvement	
Top Priority	**Secondary Priority**
Market Leadership (All)	Corporate Citizenship (All)
Customer Focus (C, F)	Management Quality (E)
Work Environment (E, CM)	Product/Service Quality (CM)
Superior Performance Areas	
Leverage Strengths	**Other Strengths**
Product/Service Quality (C, E, F)	Customer Focus (CM)
Customer Focus (E)	Work Environment (C, F)
Management Quality (C, F, CM)	Financial Performance (All)

FIGURE 7.5   Presenting Survey Priorities to Corporate Teams

Taking Extended Stakeholders Through the Gates of Engagement

The previous examples of reputation measurement results would indicate where your company stands in the minds of important constituents and also would identify reputation issues. But in seeking answers to these issues and what actions to take, it is important also to consider the state of your relationship with each segment. In other words, plan your next communications and public relations efforts in light of extended stakeholders' four gates of engagement with your firm. Let's say, for example, that reputation scores were given by suppliers, community leaders, and local media. We would recommend that your teams plan any new initiatives or changes for each segment by discussing the research implications and also by considering the following points for each of the gates.

Gate One: Awareness

- To what degree did groups answer on the survey "don't know" or "no answer" to reputation attributes? This indicates lack of awareness of your company and the need to promote more recognition.
- Are there other stakeholder segments or sub-segments that warrant special communications/public relations efforts because they have either grown in their influence or been overlooked? (One common example here may be Hispanic leaders, who increasingly should be sought out by many businesses in U.S. communities, in keeping with the growth of this segment of the population).

Gate Two: Knowledge

- What recent new programs or products/services restructuring should be brought to the attention of this segment?
- Does evidence that they have only a surface knowledge of your company and what it does warrant a special education/public relations campaign?

Gate Three: Admiration

- Are there any new awards or other testimonials your company has received that could be shared with the segment to enhance their commitment?
- Are the various segments aware of the corporate community activities or other socially responsible activities of the organization?

Gate Four: Action

- Have you considered creating advisory council(s) made up of stakeholder segment members, for example, community leaders who would advise the firm regarding employment and recruitment?
- Are there individuals or groups that can be asked to collaborate with the firm in community affairs, or even to appear in/be quoted in corporate communications, such as website information, commercials, or public service ads sponsored by the firm?
- Can you involve stakeholders more directly in your recruiting and outplacement activities?

It's Not Getting Any Easier. . .

One of the most current imperatives for tracking corporate reputation is the impact of the Internet on stakeholder communications. One of our marketing professionals recently researched a large company with which he was not very familiar and suddenly found himself linked into a chat room of investors who were posting various comments regarding this firm's management and financial performance. There was no apparent editing being done to these postings, as this was apparently an independent website, and some were extremely harsh criticisms of the CEO and other senior executives of the organization. The chance to express contempt toward a company has become easy, loose, and dangerous, given access to online audiences.

Worse than online chatter is an incident reported one day in August 2000. A well-respected, high-flying technology firm, billed as the world's largest supplier of fiber channel adapters (network equipment), had to deal with a bogus press release to an online news service, *Internet Wire*, stating that Emulex's CEO had resigned, that its third-quarter results just reported were to be restated, and that the firm was being investigated by the SEC—all of which statements were patently false.[14] The company issued an immediate and swift repudiation, but by mid-morning their stock had incredibly tumbled 62 percent on the NASDAQ stock market before trading was halted. Once people had time to calm down and absorb the truth, trading resumed, and by the close of that day, the stock had recovered to within just a few points of where it had been. Paul Folino, CEO of Emulex, was in no mood that afternoon to joke around that "reports of his demise were greatly exaggerated," but he did comment, "You'd like to think that all you need to do is continue to focus on your business, but unfortunately from time to time something like this happens. It is a message to everybody [stakeholders] to just be cautious in what you look at and do your homework before you react."[15]

There is a message here as well that it isn't enough to simply "focus on your business," unless that includes focusing on your stakeholders and being aware of all the downsides of the Internet communications available to them. An item mentioned in the same report[16] was another example in April 1999, in which stock manipulation sent Pair-Gain Technologies, Inc., up more than 30 percent when a former employee put out a false news story on the Internet that the firm was about to be taken over; the culprit was caught and pleaded guilty to two counts of securities fraud.

New risks are arising every day that require a greater need to be in touch with stakeholders and to take precautions. Are executives alert to this problem? In the Hill and Knowlton research mentioned previously, six out of ten executives expressed concern about negative information on their companies in cyberspace, but only one out of ten was actually monitoring the Internet regularly to keep abreast of what was being posted.[17]

The nature of the CEO concerns really had more to do with unhappy customers posting their dissatisfaction online. But the Internet is open to all stakeholders. Many CEOs are critical of their own websites and recognize that corporate reputation requires strong support by impressions given to those using the website of the firm. This recognition should be broadened to account for what may be communicated about them on other websites as well.

To plan and manage corporate reputation effectively across the various stakeholders that an organization deems strategically important, client organizations, PR firms, and trade associations agree that an effective form of reputation measurement is needed. Utilities, which are experiencing deregulation and must focus on their corporate brand and image as never before, are taking some leadership in this endeavor, as shown in the following case study.

•••

Case in Point: Edison International[18]

Managers at Edison International make no apologies to shareholders for spending money on local communities. Social responsibility, the managers say, has become a cornerstone of corporate strategy. The $10-billion energy concern based in Rosemead, California, spends $20 million each year on community programs such as promoting energy efficiency among households and businesses and fielding a corps of employee volunteers who have donated several hundred thousand hours of work to community and nonprofit organizations. The goal is to be devoted to corporate citizenship, but they also expect to boost reputation and in turn to attract high-quality individuals to work at, invest in, and buy from the company.

Many managers in industry today doubt that spending on social programs can deliver such benefits. The managers at Edison are no exception. They constantly question: "Is our investment in the community paying off?" They wonder if all their good works prompt, say, politicians to recommend Edison as a workplace, or move community-based organizations to recommend Edison as a place to buy when utility markets are deregulated, or influence educators to laud the firm as financially sound.

In 1998, Edison sought to find the answers to these questions. The firm surveyed local customers, business groups, educators, community organizations, and politicians to gauge the impact of its social spending. What Edison found was that most people rated the company's reputation much higher than utilities nationally and on a par with the most admired of U.S. companies. But the company wasn't the crème de la crème. Two groups—community-based organizations and educators—ranked Edison's reputation significantly below that of the most admired firms in the United States.

What actions should Edison take? To find out, managers dug deeper. They found that the main driver of the company's reputation—in the eyes of every stakeholder—was the quality of its products and services. A secondary driver was its handling of corporate social activity. A third-tier driver, in the eyes of community-based organizations, was treatment of the environment and labor practices.

The study confirmed the value of Edison's payout for social programs. Volunteers donating 700,000 hours of work to community organizations, a nationally recognized program to support minority vendors, New Era Awards for K–12 students, a community arts program, and many other programs boosted the firm's reputation for acting in the interest of the community. But the reason the company was not rated "outstanding" was that many people in the community didn't know about these good works. As a result, only one-third of key publics (leaders of community organizations, educators, government officials) ranked the firm as having one of the best overall corporate reputations. The company simply was not getting credit where credit was probably due.

Responding to the middling overall numbers, Edison intensified communications efforts—integrating its message about social programs into existing newsletters, TV ads, and its website. It also launched a new brochure and a biennial community report. Meanwhile, it fine-tuned programs to enhance even further its relationships with community stakeholders, assuring that it allocated its limited social dollars to maximum benefit.

....

Connecting Outside the Organization

Extended stakeholders bring new perspective to business and remind us of how fragile a reputation can be. Spending time with people outside our organizations also reminds us how much business people, with their mix of skills developed in the commercial world, can help solve some other problems in society if we can get them involved. The opportunities for corporate citizenship are almost endless, and these outside connections can definitely energize the inner components of your business. We explore corporate citizenship in greater detail in the next chapter.

8 Charging Up with Corporate Citizenship

elief in corporate citizenship begins with the premise that since companies make demands on workers and others in their communities, then it is good for those firms to share some of the fruits of success with others in need. In short, citizenship is when business leaders become determined to "give something back."

The art of succeeding in business with our given "family" of stakeholders—owners and investors, customers and employees, and extended stakeholders, including community leaders, suppliers, financial analysts, government officials, and other opinion leaders—hinges on motivating people's support. Financial discipline attracts capital. But to carry out business plans, we must earn stakeholders' trust before we can ask them for support and even sacrifices.

We have said that people want to be associated with good companies and, in turn, avoid ones with tainted reputations or policies and practices they disagree with. Archie B. Carroll, the Robert W. Scherer Professor of Management at the University of Georgia, has researched corporate ethics and social responsibility extensively. Adapting Carroll's concept of a "pyramid of corporate social responsibility"[1] and based on our own conclusions in this book as well, it seems clear that there is a hierarchy of being "good":

1. Good companies begin from a foundation of performance. A company must have a winning business model and strategy, then be able to execute it.
2. Company leadership must have strong core values and integrity to earn the trust of employees and other stakeholders.
3. On this platform of performance and integrity, the leading firms will reach out to offer a portion of their corporate resources to specific causes and communities in need. Such outreach, in the form of donations or volunteer help, can be called corporate citizenship.

Who Says We Must Be Good Citizens?

One might ask, does a corporation really owe something to people (beyond its owners and those with whom it has contractual obligations)? Armed with some data, we would respectfully respond to that question with another one: "Is there anyone who *doesn't* think that successful businesses should 'give something back'?" In a 1996 *BusinessWeek*/Lou Harris poll, the response was overwhelming: 95 percent of the 1,000 adults surveyed believed that U.S. companies do owe something to their workers and the communities in which they operate. More specifically, survey participants felt that businesses should sacrifice some profit to make life a bit better for their workers and communities.[2]

This notion of "giving back" is frequently heard from celebrities in entertainment and professional sports who, by nature, rarely "hide their light under a bushel" when supporting their profession or worthy causes. But despite the inevitable publicity, reaction from the public tends to support their cause-related endeavors as being positive and admirable.

NFL quarterback Peyton Manning, only a third-year player with the Indianapolis Colts but definitely a rising star in the league, has initiated the Peyback Foundation. With local sponsors, including a children's hospital, Manning and his foundation held the "Peyback Classic," inviting area high school teams to play a regular-season game inside the RCA Dome on a Saturday in August 2000; all proceeds benefited the Indianapolis Public Schools athletic programs. The newspaper promotion tag line explained the program's rationale thus: "Peyton Manning thinks every high school player should get a chance to play like the pros, even if just for one game."[3]

Even from celebrities, the most impressive aspect of charitable giving is the fact that it is voluntary. Businesses absolutely must pay their taxes and are virtually forced to "contribute" to investors and owners. Thus, voluntary giving by a company becomes something special. And most stakeholders love it—they want to see businesses reaching out beyond their own self-interest and finding ways to "pay back" by helping others.

The Meaning of Giving

There are various ways of giving back that fit under the title "corporate citizenship." The Council on Foundations, a Washington, D.C., association of foundations and corporations serving the public by promoting effective philanthropy, defines corporate citizenship as, "charitable cash contributions, contributions of products and services, volunteerism, and other business transactions that a company voluntarily undertakes to support a cause, issue, or non-profit organization."[4] The variety of ways in which organizations invest in good corporate citizenship range from giving away money to making in-kind gifts of products or services to involving employees in good causes on company time.

The impact that those types of corporate voluntary efforts have on the direct recipients, on those involved in delivering the services (employees), and on the greater community becomes a unifying dynamic across different stakeholder groups. As when the diverse inhabitants of a major city pull together behind a championship home sports team, far-flung workers and other stakeholders are unified as they work alongside each other on common causes. Depending on the cause your firm is involved with, employees might be linked with members of the outside community or even with competitors holding similar values, bringing greater connectivity between stakeholder groups. Corporate citizenship offers other benefits as well, but it begins with the integration and unity of stakeholders.

The Tradition of Giving

Part of the reason people in the United States love to see corporate philanthropy may be because it has long been part of the culture. Small towns across the country have preserved their libraries built in the early twentieth century with Andrew Carnegie's money. *Time* magazine reports the results of a survey by the Johns Hopkins Comparative Non-Profit Sector Project indicating that Americans give more time and money to charities than any other country participating in the study (73 percent of Americans do so). The total for charitable gifts by Americans is reported to have been $190 billion in 1999, equal to about one-third of the domestic federal budget, or 2 percent of the nation's income. This figure is the highest level of giving in 28 years, reflecting a newfound generosity accompanying new wealth.[5]

The spirit of charity and volunteerism in the United States doesn't give this country a lock on corporate unselfishness in the world, however. In fact, out of five firms recognized for their "social consciousness" among *IndustryWeek's* "Best Managed Companies in 1999," three were from outside the United States:[6]

- Novartis AG, based in Switzerland—The company has spearheaded education programs in Sri Lanka that teach early signs and treatment of leprosy and has sustained this program for 10 years. Half of those afflicted with leprosy are now seeking treatment on their own, compared with just 9 percent when the program began. The company also encourages employees to raise funds to prevent blindness by holding walk-a-thons. Finally, they plant vegetable gardens contributing to food banks and assist in literacy campaigns.

- Cadbury Schweppes PLC, based in Great Britain and Canada—Employees recycle soft drink bottles in Central Africa, channeling proceeds into educational projects. To support the Easter Seal Research Institute, which studies the physical disabilities of children, Cadbury Canada initiated the Great Bunny Mall Tour and the Chocolate Challenge to raise funds. In India, Cadbury's Doorstep project offers children from deprived areas basic educational services.

- Denso Corporation, based in Japan—The company operates a volunteer support center in Japan that helps the elderly and handicapped, works to protect the environment, and directs youth sports. Employees also conduct clothing-collection drives every spring and fall for the needy in developing nations. One business unit, the Denso Taiyo Co. Ltd., employs more than 200 physically disabled people in assembly instrument clusters.

The top giver in the United States currently is the Bill and Melinda Gates Foundation, with the remarkable figure of $22 billion given or pledged over the past five years. The Gates Foundation sees its mission as finding cures for diseases in the developing world and targets its donations to international vaccination and children's health programs. (Third World illnesses exist in part because there is no economy to underwrite research or the ensuing treatments and drugs.)

The Foundation is investing about $400 million annually in global health projects. Finding a vaccine for malaria is a top priority, with a general focus on creating new vaccines and cures and making them available to those who need them the most and can least afford them.

Because of the Foundation's unique focus and streamlined giving process, it is able to operate with just 25 employees, a lean staff compared to other large foundations.[7]

Not only Gates but many other successful technology entrepreneurs also are applying lessons learned from their businesses to their philanthropy—namely, ensuring that charitable investments wind up helping their ultimate "customers," those in need, without wasting money through a filter of bureaucracy and red tape. These entrepreneurs are posing challenges to charitable organizations, which in some cases will have to make changes to prove they can effectively deploy the new donations to the expectations of the givers. For one thing, recipients can be expected to measure results more than just measuring levels of giving.

It's not just high-visibility people who make charitable contributions. In the United States, it's hard not to know people who volunteer time and money to their local school boards, churches, Little League, Scouting, and other organizations. As retired General Colin Powell said, "Let's not just praise billionaires. This has been (our) culture—moms and pops who are volunteering as Big Brothers and Big Sisters and running the Boy Scouts and the Junior Achievement."[8] In fact, 85 percent of all funds donated in the United States comes from individuals.

Certainly numerous companies are making contributions as well. A 1999 Cone/Roper study on corporate citizenship reports that more than half of all U.S. workers say their employers contribute to social causes.[9] *Giving USA* was quoted as the source in "The Chronicle of Philanthropy" for a total of over $143 billion given in 1997, $21.5 billion by foundations or corporations.[10] Just considering individuals or organizations making grants to worthy projects through foundations, the Council on Foundations has reported nearly 1,700 members giving a total of almost $8 billion in 1998 (see Table 8.1).[11]

Certain corporations not only give generously but hold their course by making longer-term commitments to particular causes. In the same Cone/Roper study mentioned previously, citizens, in fact, want companies to make commitments that are long-term as well as

TABLE 8.1   Council on Foundations, 1998 Grantmaking Levels of Members

Grantmaking Level	Number of Members	Total Grants on Record
Less than $100,000	343	$10,119,574
$100,000 to $499,999	474	$127,069,966
500,000 to $999,999	244	$175,270,539
$1 million to $4.9 million	376	$841,901,091
$5 million to $9.9 million	103	$743,691,644
$10 million or more	147	$6,035,044,109
TOTAL	1,687	$7,933,096,923

Source: Council on Foundations website,
http://www/cof.org/membersonly/NewWindowview.cfm?path=/membersonly/
membershipinfo/1998stats/AssestsGrants/Assetsgrants.htm.

substantive to important social issues. Nearly eight in ten participants said they preferred a company that would commit to one cause for a long period of time rather than a variety of causes for shorter time periods. Reported in the same study were some examples of programs that had been supported for some duration (see Table 8.2)[12]:

Payback for Payback

Why do business leaders decide to make substantial contributions of cash, employees' time, or in-kind products and services to charitable causes? And are their reasons really altruistic or merely practical? In other words, do companies give strictly because it's the right thing to do, or do they feel they will be ultimately repaid for their good deeds by the marketplace?

The answer captures some of both options, but we would give some weight to business leaders' sincere belief in the causes rather than just thinking of the return. And realistically, there are certainly plenty of other ways to invest in corporate promotion and advertising than "cause-marketing." In fact, a 1996 Council on Foundations/ Walker Information study reported that 90 percent of consumers couldn't recall specific philanthropic efforts by companies.[13]

TABLE 8.2   Programs Supported by Corporations for Lengthy Periods

Program	In Place Since ...	Program Sponsor
Ronald McDonald House Charities	1974	McDonalds
Bookit!	1985	Pizza Hut
Give the Gift of Sight	1988	LensCrafters
Team Depot	1989	The Home Depot
Breast Cancer Awareness Crusade	1993	Avon

Source: "The 1999 Cone/Roper Cause Related Trends Report," presented at the Special Olympics Marketing Conference, Arlington, VA, May 2, 2000.

Instead of supporting a cause, businesses could reinvest their money in avenues such as new technology or hiring new talent for growth, or even choosing to sponsor sporting events or to have their names associated with skyscrapers or convention and sports facilities. Companies may indeed hope for some ultimate payback for their "giving back" to worthy causes, but it's hard to say that their hearts are not in the right place when they have selected this form of contribution over other investments. Bill Gates was quoted in *Time* reflecting on the issue of world health in the midst of his other pressing issues: "The more people know about this—about the millions of lives that can be saved, about the millions of children who are dying of diseases every year that we have cures for—then how can you not do something about it? The most important priority to me is saying we could save millions of lives a year."[14]

However, the fact that most organizations want their names associated with the cause they are supporting makes it safe to assume they don't mind accruing some benefit from their philanthropy. Companies give in part because it's the right thing to do, but they are willing to accept and even promote practical benefits from their contributions. Those benefits might include:

- The organization and its brand becoming associated with a particular cause.

- The firm's reputation being enhanced over time, becoming known as a company that makes charitable contributions.
- Employees being more content working for an organization that gives to good causes, and/or enjoying participating directly in company-sponsored activities.
- Communities and opinion leaders treating organizations more favorably in the course of other issues such as tax abatement requests or real estate purchases because of the company's support of the community.
- Customers being more inclined to purchase products and services from corporations associated with charitable giving.
- Investors feeling good about owning a stake in a firm that supports causes in which they believe.
- Healthier societies and cultures ultimately providing more viable markets worldwide for services and products.

The essence of good business practices is accurate accounting, and just as more requirements are being asked of nonprofits administering charitable projects or the foundations giving grants, corporate gift administrators want to account for any ensuing benefit back to their own organizations. Eventually, such information may increasingly be requested by boards of directors and institutional investors.

Business owners and leaders want to measure the effectiveness of anything to which the organization devotes its resources. Tim Mc-Climon, Executive Director of the AT&T Foundation and a member of the board of directors of the Council on Foundations, put it this way: "Corporate giving programs have had to be more accountable for helping to achieve business objectives as well as philanthropic objectives."[15]

Evidence That Demands
Good Corporate Citizenship

An updated set of evidence regarding the impact of corporate citizenship on business performance has been assembled as the Measur-

ing the Business Value of Corporate Philanthropy project,[16] which
Walker Information conducted for the Council on Foundations. This
project underwrote a special discovery process in 1999, with a literature search of studies regarding the impact of corporate citizenship.
The discovery phase was accomplished by Archie Carroll and Kim
Davenport. Some of the most important findings from the literature
search follow:

1. "Corporate Philanthropy and Business Performance," by
   David Lewin and J. M. Sabater, published in *Corporate
   Philanthropy at the Crossroads*: This study combined survey
   questionnaire data on company/community involvement and
   employees with the financial performance data from
   Standard & Poor's COMPUSTAT files. The major conclusion
   was that community involvement has an impact on business
   performance, employee morale also has an impact on
   business performance, and a combination of community
   involvement and employee morale has an even stronger
   association with business performance.
2. "The Link Between Corporate Citizenship and Financial
   Performance," by Steven J. Garone, reported in the
   Conference Board research report of the same title. The
   findings actually reference an earlier Conference Board study
   by Myra Alperson, entitled "Building the Corporate
   Community Economic Development Team, 1994," which
   found that businesses do not invest in community projects
   for economic development strictly for immediate financial
   gain. But they do have immediate business goals that are
   "softer" in nature:
   - To enhance corporate image: 99 percent
   - To develop trust in the company: 98 percent
   - To develop local talent: 93 percent
   - To support programs with specific goals/impacts: 87
     percent
   - To improve ability to recruit: 85 percent

3. "Corporate Social Performance and Organizational Attractiveness to Perspective Employees," by Daniel Turban and Daniel W. Greening, reported in the *Academy of Management Journal,* June 1997, found that "corporate social performance" (CSP) is related positively to a company's reputation and to its attractiveness as an employer, suggesting that a firm's CSP could provide a competitive advantage.

4. "Corporate Citizenship: Cultural Antecedents and Business Benefits," by Isabell Maignan, O. C. Ferrell, and G. Tomas M. Hult, *Journal of the Academy of Marketing Science*, Fall 1999—Pro-active corporate citizenship was found to have potential business value. Being an active corporation in citizenship activities is associated with enhanced levels of employee commitment, customer loyalty, and business performance as evaluated in terms of assets, return on investments, profits growth, and sales growth.

5. "The Corporate Social Performance—Financial Performance Link," by Sandra Waddock and Samuel B. Graves, *Strategic Management Journal*, 1997—This study, which examined relationships between corporate social performance and the financial performance of 465 U.S. companies across a broad range of industries, found that:

   • Strong social performance was associated with return on assets at a very significant level.

   • Strong social performance was associated with return on sales at a significant level.

   • Some studies determined at best a weak or inconclusive relationship between social performance and financial performance. (There were even studies showing a negative relationship, although these examples tended to be found when corporate illegalities or product problems such as recalls did not drive stock values down as much as hypothesized.)

In this discovery phase, Carroll and Davenport also summarized an important study previously mentioned, the 1999 Cone/Roper "Cause-Related Trends Report." (Cone, Inc., headquartered in Boston, is a branding and communications firm developing and implementing cause and strategic philanthropy programs; Roper Starch is a New York based, full-service firm conducting both marketing and opinion studies in the United States and worldwide.)

This nationwide study looked at a cross-section of approximately 2,000 adult men and women who were interviewed in their homes face-to-face in August 1998. Key findings related to corporate citizenship are discussed below.

Corporate Citizenship Enhances Corporate Image[17]

- More than eight in ten Americans have a positive image of companies that support a cause they care about.
- This positive image of companies committed to a cause is even higher among a group the researchers broke out as being opinion leaders, based on their higher-than-average social and political activities.
- Acceptability of cause programs as a business practice is on the increase over the past five years.
- Two out of three citizens report greater trust in companies that are aligned with social issues.

Corporate Citizenship Inspires More Active Support from Stakeholders[18]

- More than half of all workers wish their employers would do more to support social causes.
- Nearly two-thirds of Americans (approximately 130 million consumers) report they would be likely to switch brands or retailers to one that is associated with a good cause when price and quality are considered equal.

- About 90 percent of workers in companies involved with a cause program are proud of their company's values, versus only 56 percent of those whose employers are not committed to a cause. (This statistic implies that employees in "cause" organizations would speak more favorably to others about their employer.)
- 87 percent of employees in "cause" companies feel a strong sense of loyalty to their employers, versus just 67 percent of employees of firms without a cause association.

Organizations Assessing Impact of Giving

The literature search made it clear that the only mitigating factors between corporate giving and business outcomes were stakeholders, especially employees, customers, and community leaders/citizens. Any organization wanting to measure business outcomes from philanthropy must seek feedback from these segments.

Lending credence to an earlier point that business governance and accounting will demand that philanthropic efforts be measured, the next phase of research sponsored by the Council on Foundations with Walker Information tested a survey tool to evaluate the awareness of and impact of charitable activities on stakeholder commitment. Doug Grisaffe, chief methodologist at Walker Information, worked with two corporate members of the Council on Foundations, using test samples with customers, employees, and "community influential" stakeholders. From his analysis of the results, Grisaffe concluded the following:[19]

- A meaningful index of key attitudes toward a company's philanthropy can be constructed from survey answers. Grisaffe developed this statistically reliable index, now called the Philanthropy Citizenship Index, or PCI, by combining the answers to three specific questions:

1. Compared to other companies, [company name] does its fair share to help the community and society.
2. Overall, [company name] is the kind of company that helps the community and society by contributing things like time, volunteers, money and sponsorships of nonprofit events and causes.
3. [Company name] really seems to care about giving and making contributions to help the community and society.

- Stakeholders definitely become aware of giving programs and initiatives and can judge their effectiveness and how well the programs fit the company's identity.
- Among each type of stakeholder, those with higher (more positive) PCIs were far more likely to
  - hold a sense of goodwill toward the firm;
  - give the firm the benefit of the doubt if it experienced negative publicity about ethical or legal practices; and
  - have customers and employees who will use the firm's record of supporting good causes as one reason for remaining loyal, if trying to decide whether to switch

- Grisaffe also concluded from the data that:
  1. the more giving initiatives that stakeholders are aware of,
  2. the more they think these programs are effective, and
  3. the more they think the programs "fit" the identify of the organization, then
  4. the more favorably they rate the organization in terms of cash giving, volunteerism, in-kind giving, and noncommercial sponsorship.

- Higher overall perceptions of corporate philanthropy lead to a greater likelihood of people acting in ways that help the company experience business success, such as staying loyal, giving recommendations, and so forth.

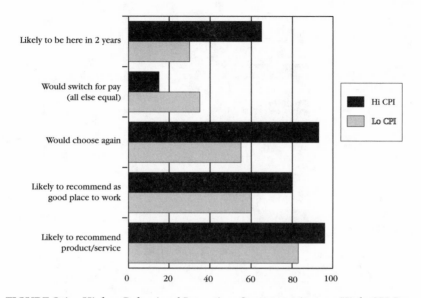

FIGURE 8.1   Higher Behavioral Intention Outcomes Among High CPI Employees
Source:"Measuring the Business Value of Corporate Philanthropy," research report by Walker Information, October 2000. Available at *Councils on Foundations* website, http://www.cof.org.

This last point should receive a great deal of attention from business people reading the results; it is evidence that philanthropy contributes to favorable business outcomes. It should be noted that the results were based on the constituents of two large, well-known corporations, one in healthcare and related financial services and the other in financial services. These companies became successful for business reasons including, but obviously extending beyond, just being generous to their communities. On the other hand, there is a strong correlation between perceptions of being a giving organization and winning commitment from stakeholders. Note in the following figures how customers are more likely (in Figure 8.1) to do business with the firm again, recommend their services to others, and so forth, when they give a high CPI score rather than a low one.

In Figure 8.2, community opinion leaders (influentials) proved much more likely to support the firm, recommend it as an invest-

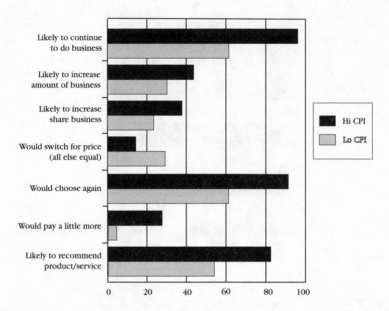

FIGURE 8.2   Higher Behavioral Intention Outcomes Among High CPI Customers

Source: "Measuring the Business Value of Corporate Philanthropy," research report
by Walker Information, October 2000. Available at *Councils on Foundations*
website, http://www.cof.org.

ment, or recommend it for employment to others when they appreci-
ated the firm's philanthropic efforts (high CPI rating).

Finally, note in Figure 8.3 that a similar story came out in employees as well as customers and community leaders. These results were
similar for each firm participating in the study.

If corporate giving recognized by constituents ultimately leads to
greater support of your organization and its products and services,
does this mean that giving should always be driven by business motives rather than just helping the recipient(s)? In a word, no. Anonymous giving is an honorable act, especially for individual donors.
Giving anonymously usually means giving selflessly, without ulterior
motives. On the other hand, there are those who can exhibit leadership when they are known to be supporters of a worthy cause, encouraging others to emulate them. People in organizations, in
particular, benefit from seeing role models involved in charitable ac-

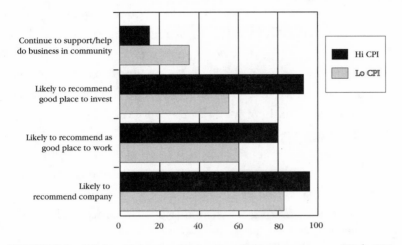

FIGURE 8.3   Higher Behavioral Intention Outcomes Among High CPI
Community Influentials
Source:"Measuring the Business Value of Corporate Philanthropy," research
report by Walker Information, October 2000. Available at *Councils on Foundations*
website, http://www.cof.org.

tivities, and business leaders can be inspired by seeing other leaders
supporting worthy causes.

What should be the most important "take-aways" from this research
on business philanthropy? Grisaffe and the Council on Foundations
have drawn some very practical implications from their research, including that companies should:

- engage in forms of corporate giving that "fit" with the identity
  of the company;
- monitor the effectiveness of the initiatives that they support;
- make sure that their stakeholders are aware of the initiatives
  they are involved with; and
- if already involved in charitable giving (whether through
  cash, volunteerism, in-kind services or products, or
  noncommercial sponsorships), measure the perceptions of
  key constituents. The study proved that stakeholder
  perceptions can be meaningfully and reliably measured using
  a simple index—the CPI.

On this last point, McClimon of the AT&T Foundation and Council on Foundations adds, "We need ways of measuring (business objectives of corporate giving). Most companies are doing ad hoc surveys and questionnaires. [At the Council on Foundations] we're seeking to give corporations a tool they can use to measure the effectiveness of programs and compare them with other corporations."[20]

In fact, the Council will be offering a "tool kit" to help organizations measure stakeholder perceptions as a way to identify the impact of philanthropic efforts on the business. The kit will contain survey versions for different stakeholders and a guidebook on administering the surveys and on interpreting the results. Companies using this kit or using a similar approach will be able to:

- Establish a baseline from which they can track progress in their corporate philanthropy "score," as perceived by major stakeholder segments.
- Break down the scores by different programs or types of giving to promote more effective use of giving resources.
- Prove to shareholders and others the strategic benefits of giving.

....

Case in Point: United Way— Fostering Stakeholder Involvement

Just as companies rely on chains of supply for distribution and sales, there are important allies for "distributing" social services to the end recipients. The United Way is one of the best-known charitable umbrella organizations, particularly in relation to fostering programs for employee involvement.

United Way of America is an enormous network of 1,400 community-based "constellations, local United Ways throughout the United States that raise donations and channel them to agencies in those communities that meet health and human-care needs. United Way was formally launched in 1963, merging what had been local Community Chest and United Fund charity organizations. Its roots actually dated back to nineteenth-century efforts in major U.S. cities to unify local charitable institutions to gain efficiencies and to protect donors.

United Way's mission is "to increase the organized capacity of people to care for one another."Volunteers do fund-raising to support local agency providers, mainly in an annual community-wide campaign.The scope of this operation is massive:"In total, voluntary contributions to United Ways support approximately 45,000 agencies and chapters, helping millions of people from all walks of life and income groups. Apart from government, United Ways support the greatest variety of health and human services in the country."[21]

With successful volunteer recruitment efforts and with help from the local employer partners, who collect payroll deductions from employee-donors, United Way keeps its administrative expenses to just 13 percent of total funds raised. (Better Business Bureau Guidelines for charities suggest that administrative expenses of up to 35 percent are acceptable.)

The United Way's proven efficiency, presence, and momentum in community fund-raising, and its effective ongoing screening and monitoring of every nonprofit, tax-exempt agency to which it channels funds, make it an attractive partner for businesses wanting to be involved in corporate citizenship.[22]

• •

Case in Point on Stakeholder Involvement: The Special Olympics

As another example, many around the world are familiar with the Special Olympics organization, which sponsors programs in 160 countries. Special Olympics officially dates back to 1968 and the First International Special Olympics Games at Soldier Field in Chicago. Founder Eunice Kennedy Shriver organized the event based on her earlier work in a day camp for individuals with mental retardation. She had observed their capabilities for developing

greater fitness, confidence, and character through sports and competition.

A 1996 study by Nye Lavalle & Associates reported in the *Chronicle of Philanthropy* cited Special Olympics as being the single
most credible social program in the minds of typical Americans, just
ahead of the Girl Scouts, Mothers Against Drunk Driving, the Boy
Scouts, and the Ronald McDonald House.[23] The goal of the organization is "for all persons with mental retardation to have the chance
to become useful and productive citizens who are accepted and re-
spected in their communities."[24]

Beyond this inspirational premise, the Special Olympics is unique
in its extremely heavy emphasis on volunteerism in proportion to
cash contributions. The organization charges no fees for training or
coaching, and spectators pay no entrance fees to attend the games.
Special Olympics claims to have more volunteers than any other
sports organization—more than 500,000. "Families are the true
backbone of Special Olympics," equipping athletes and events with
volunteers.[25]

But corporations are becoming increasingly involved as sponsors
for the program, supplying not only funding but also employee
time to volunteer for preparation and running events. The organization offers these types of activities to sponsor companies:

- Special Olympics training programs as employee fitness
  programs
- Enabling and encouraging employees to participate in local
  Special Olympics programs
- Starting Unified Sports programs to generate interaction
  between employees with and without mental retardation in
  integrated workplaces

A new program called Team is part of the strategy to align the
Special Olympics organization with corporate partners, much as it
has partnered in the past with some of the world's best-known en-
tertainers, professional athletes, and political leaders. Corporate
sponsors have included ABB Inc., Oracle Corp., Fleet Bank, Phoenix
Home Life, AMF, and Coca-Cola. Although the organization already

claims to be serving more than a million athletes, opportunities exist for hundreds of millions more to become participants if additional volunteers and funds become available; for this reason, Special Olympics is working to grow its corporate partnerships.[26]

. . . .

Corporate Giving Taps into Exponential Power of Integrated Stakeholder Relationships

Participating companies have found the experience of working with Special Olympics and other causes to be a unifying one within their own organizations—across work teams and between labor and management, customers and communities, investors and the general public. People come together to participate in common causes, especially those mentioned previously that carry enormous credibility. The organizations that partner with United Way, Special Olympics, and other worthwhile social causes experience the dynamic of engaging not just one stakeholder group but multiple ones. Employees, customers, investors, and local citizens feel more integral to a company that has involved itself and its people above and beyond just doing their jobs; this involvement in turn seems to earn the company favorable word-of-mouth—employee ambassadorship, if you will—by workers demonstrating pride in their employer when they talk to customers, prospective employees, opinion leaders, and the general public.

. . . .

Case in Point: The Perils of the "Mission Firm" Exemplified by Ben and Jerry's

A few commercial firms are so linked with their social activity or mission that it seems to be as important to them as the business itself. Ben and Jerry's, based in South Burlington, Vermont, is one of the best-known examples of a firm combining business success not only with a uniquely fun and philanthropic culture, but with one that has become socially and politically active as well. The company story has almost become enshrined in modern American culture.

Boyhood chums Ben Cohen and Jerry Greenfield completed a correspondence course in ice cream making and opened their first store in a renovated Burlington gas station in 1978. Within a few years, they had learned to distribute their ice cream product in pint containers through local groceries and had sold their first franchise. A huge turning point for the fledgling firm came in 1981 when *Time* magazine acclaimed their product "the best ice cream in the world." In 1984, the company went public and sales were over $4 million. Clearly, Ben and Jerry's was destined to be a success, offering a superb product in an era of yuppie-driven demand for the best in quality merchandise.

But in addition to its great-tasting ice cream flavors, Ben and Jerry's became known as being a different kind of company. For one thing, the founders were self-professed ex-hippies of the 1970s. Living in a college town, their business savvy and success was accompanied by counterculture irreverence and quirky humor, and their corporate environment reflected it. Witness that one of their most popular flavors was named "Cherry Garcia" after the (now deceased) leader of the Grateful Dead and that their public relations events are likely to involve hot air balloons, personal appearances by the founders, and free ice cream. When Ben Cohen stepped down as CEO in 1995, the company engaged a search firm but also ran a 100-word essay contest under the headline, "Yo! I want to be CEO!" The winning prize was not only the job but a lifetime supply of ice cream.

But being a different company under Cohen and Greenfield meant more than just being funky, wacky, and fun—it meant having a "social mission." In 1985, the company formed the Ben and Jerry Foundation, pledging 7.5 percent of pre-tax profits annually for community support and other forms of giving. Since 1988, according to its own website, these activities have followed a statement of mission, including fostering social change by helping fund community activist organizations and encouraging responsible environmental practices. A *Wall Street Journal* article recently summed up Ben and Jerry's stated philosophy: "To operate the company in a way that actively recognizes the central role that business plays in the structure of society by initiating . . . ways to improve the quality of life of a broad community—local, national and international. Social issues of concern include preserving family farms and working to rid paper products of Dioxin."[27]

What is most striking about this mission is its sheer breadth:"improve quality of life . . . local, national and international." Is there any better way to say that one's mission is to "change the world?" In addition to setting extremely high expectations, this statement implies not only community support, but social change. Evoking social change requires taking political positions on policy making, and any company choosing political positions outside of industry issues will find that at least some stakeholders are either politically opposed or neutral in their beliefs on these issues. In their book, *Ben & Jerry's Double-Dip, How to Run a Values-Led Business and Make Money, Too,* Cohen and Greenfield admit that political stands against such actions as military expenditures and the flooding of Native Indian lands for a hydro-electric plant have either alienated or puzzled some customers, employees, and others.[28] At the time of this writing, a donation attributed to Ben and Jerry's for a particular political cause has led to an active boycott of Ben and Jerry's products promoted by one opposing interest group on the Web.

In addition to gaining detractors, taking such stands does win intense loyalty among like-minded supports. In Ben and Jerry's case, some people undoubtedly eat their ice cream, choose to work there, and/or buy their stock at least in part because they share their philosophy of social activism. This fervency was visible early in February 2000 when a group of "socially responsible" business people, including Anita Roddick, founder of Body Shop International PLC, were among the final bidders jockeying to buy Ben and Jerry's Homemade, Inc. The purchase was ultimately made, however, by Unilever NV, the Anglo-Dutch conglomerate with consumer product brands including Ragu spaghetti sauce and Pepsodent toothpaste. Unilever's solo bid, reported to have been $43.60 a share, topped the final bid by the socially concerned group (in which Unilever interestingly was also a part at a 28 percent stake), which offered $38 a share, but then withdrew the offer for reasons unstated.[29]

According to the *Wall Street Journal*, the final agreement with Unilever was negotiated to have Ben and Jerry's CEO, Perry Odak, retain financial and operational control of the firm, while Cohen and Greenfield would control the "social mission and brand integrity," continuing the firm's involvement in "critical, global economic social missions." The deal included some unique conditions: that milk supplies would continue to be purchased from Vermont dairy farmers at above-market prices, that the 7.5 percent of pre-tax profit-donation was sacrosanct, and that Mr. Cohen would receive $5 million to start a venture-capital fund for investments in low-income communities. As a postscript to the deal consummated in early 2000, Perry Odak by November 2000 was reported to be stepping down as CEO to spend more time with his family. He supported Unilever's decision to bring in Ives Couette, an executive with Unilever's international ice cream operation, to be the next Ben and Jerry's CEO. This was not the choice, however, of Cohen and Greenfield, who lobbied for the slot to go to a food service executive from a different company, who was a longtime member of Ben and Jerry's board. In their written statement, they acknowledged Unilever's right to run the company, but said their candidate had the "clear and established' social commitment and added ominously, "We have not decided whether or not to remain with the company."[30]

By early December 2000, a consumer advocate effort on behalf of Ben and Jerry's was underway. Maynard, Massachusetts–based SaveBenandJerry.com, which had actually been organized with 17,000 individual Ben and Jerry's fans as members before the company was sold to Unilever, was being revitalized for this battle to name the CEO. Rather than asking people to boycott Unilever, they urged writing/e-mailing the leaders of the firm.[31] Ben Cohen now made it clear that he would quit unless a co-CEO was named who was immersed in the social mission of the company. Both the departing Ben and Jerry's CEO Odak and Unilever officials were quick to point out, however, that Unilever had lived up to its side of the agreement, including supporting their social and philanthropic ideals.[32]

Garrett LaPorto, who leads the outside protest effort, was quoted as saying, "We're going to leverage the anti-corporate movement that took root in Seattle. There are millions who detest corporate practices and look to Ben and Jerry's to lead a different way."[33] This statement illustrates just how high the expectations became for Ben and Jerry's to be "a different company." Those kinds of expectations may have little chance of being fulfilled with the change in the control of the company, but the final chapters of that story have yet to be written.

Ben and Jerry's is just one of a number of firms that, beyond being just involved in corporate citizenship, define their entire strategy around the "mission," with the mission being somewhat broad and associated with social change. Many firms more easily identify with a narrow mission that closely fits their business and professional expertise. Merck focuses on the health of patients, finding that theme easy to focus its philanthropy on as well as its business planning. Likewise, LensCrafters, the eyeglass provider, which is discussed at length in the next chapter, centers its giving efforts with its business plan: to help people see better.

Can companies overdo it? Can they be overly concerned regarding their philanthropic missions to the detriment of their business performance? Let us first say emphatically that, for the vast majority of companies, the bigger issue is overlooking the opportunities to be giving more, not overdoing it. On the other hand, almost anything can be overdone, including a business being inordinately socially active. We do not want to judge any institution unfairly, particularly "early leaders" or true believers in philanthropy. At the same time, there are some lessons to be learned from the case of Ben and Jerry's and from other firms very strongly associated with "doing good."

Don't let the social mission distract you from the business mission. Business success is the foundation and enabler for making socially responsible commitments. Ben and Jerry's Homemade has generally performed well in recent years, although it did hit the wall on profit-making in 1995, prompting the infamous search for an outside CEO. (The person hired in that campaign only lasted one year.) More recently, the company obviously was seeking needed distribution channels and capital at the time it was sold to Unilever.

To maintain some separation between their business management and the effective oversight of their philanthropic missions, many corporations benefit from working with alliance partners such as the United Way, Red Cross, Special Olympics, or other nonprofits. The philanthropic ally not only guides the giving activities but can participate in mutual "cause marketing," making various audiences aware of their collaboration to the benefit of both parties.

Keep the social mission somewhat specific or targeted, and ideally, a fit with your business. A targeted mission helps in managing people's expectations regarding what can be done as well as in deciding what types and sources of giving to be involved with. Employee respondents in the Council on Foundations survey were more impressed by corporate philanthropy when it seemed to be a good fit with the company and its business. Merck and LensCrafters again are good examples of crafting a fit between philanthropy and business strategies.

The more we make claims to be a good corporate citizen, the more we must watch our back for accusations of hypocrisy. Anyone claiming to know what is "good" or "right" becomes a target if caught doing anything that even appears to be the opposite.

For example, firms get acquired every day, but when Ben and Jerry's announced it was talking to an international conglomerate, it raised eyebrows and made news because its most fervent supporters "detest corporate practices." Perry Odak, brought in by Ben and Jerry's as a very capable CEO, had previously headed up U.S. Repeating Arms (maker of Winchester rifles). This made Ben and Jerry's Homemade open to criticism and ridicule because of its prior support of gun control. And we won't even get into whether consuming super premium ice cream every day meets basic health wellness standards for many consumers! We don't mean to pick on Ben and Jerry's, an American business icon and one of the more interesting business stories anywhere. But the company's form of visible activist stance does set it up for criticism when it continues to have to make hard business decisions.

Ben and Jerry's isn't the only company that paid a price when the business was a platform to espouse broader ideas for social change and justice. Anita Roddick, founder of the Body Shop, the Brighton, England–based franchiser of quality skin and health care products with more than 1,700 stores in 48 countries, helped create the growing niche of natural-based or "green" personal products. In addition to battles for environmental protection and against animal testing, Roddick has been highly visible in speaking against centralized multinational corporations (because they are decentralized through franchising, she differentiates the Body Shop from that category).

Ralph Nader once said, "Anita (Roddick) is the most progressive business person I know." With such a high profile established not only for doing good but for making things better for everyone, it was probably only a matter of time until perceived inconsistencies between the company's operations and its image were pointed out. Investigative journalist Jon Entine, former producer of *NBC Nightly News* and ABC's *20/20,* was among the first to do that when "Shattered Myth" was published by *Business Ethics* magazine in late 1994. One of the Body Shop's inconsistencies noted in the article was that speaking against animal testing is apparently much easier than never using animal-tested ingredients in personal care products. The Body Shop didn't test products on animals itself, but apparently did still use ingredients that had been animal-tested.[34]

Make no mistake that philanthropic efforts and employee involvement can certainly reward a firm with favorable exposure as well. Both Ben and Jerry's and the Body Shop have received far more favorable exposure than negative in trade journals and mass media, as far as we could tell. Unleashing stakeholder power in that way, in fact, grabs the attention of third parties who evaluate and honor deserving firms based on higher exemplary management practices and business culture. The following case from *IndustryWeek's* "Best Managed Com-

panies in 1999" demonstrates how the social involvement of corporations has come to the forefront in assessing effective business management.[35]

••

Case in Point: General Mills

Many families on a busy day might partake of a bowl of Cheerios in
the morning, a Nature Valley granola bar after lunch, and a quick
meal of Hamburger Helper in the evening. Considering that all
three of these well-known products are made by General Mills, it's
not surprising that this consumer product giant has long targeted
its social outreach "to strengthen families and promote a safe, nurturing environment for children and youth," according to Reatha
Clark King, president of the General Mills Foundation.[36] What is surprising and impressive is the breadth and depth of this firm's commitment to corporate citizenship. *IndustryWeek* (IW) showcased
General Mills in its special article, "IW's 100 Best-Managed Companies" in August 1999:

> General Mills Inc. has been one of the top 10 companies in return-
> on-equity among the "IW 1000" since 1996. But that solid financial
> performance alone isn't why—it also has been chosen as one of
> "IW's Best-Managed Companies" for four straight years. *Rather, it is
> General Mills' social conscience and high involvement of its em-
> ployees in such issues—80% of its employees and 40% of its re-
> tirees are engaged in volunteer activities each year—that makes
> it a best-managed company.*[37]

In just the last five years of the twentieth century, General Mills'
community giving programs donated 76 million pounds of food,
plus $155 million of contributions targeting hunger, education for
students, safe neighborhoods, and start-up enterprises that can create jobs.

One example of the company's giving was in May 2000, months
after the IW recognition, during the raging forest fires in Los
Alamos, New Mexico. Thousands of donated granola bars fed hun-

gry firefighters, 11,000 boxes of cereal manufactured just 100 miles away in Albuquerque were sent over to feed displaced families, and the General Mills Foundation contributed $25,000 in emergency assistance to the local Red Cross.[38]

IW reported other General Mills examples, such as a monthly community meeting in a tough north Minneapolis neighborhood involving residents, business people, and public officials. The meetings were later linked to major decreases in crime, vandalism, and crack houses, and a growth in youth programs and improved hope in what had been a tense, discouraged community.

Washington, D.C.–based Social Compact recognized General Mills in 1999 for supporting Siyeza, a frozen food start-up company in northern Minneapolis. General Mills provided $1.5 million in interest-free loans and hundreds of free consulting hours; in late 1999 Siyeza had created 36 jobs in the inner city.[39] By June 2000, when General Mills received the Ron Brown Award from the Conference Board for the Siyeza project, Siyeza was providing 200 jobs and generating more than $10 million in sales.[40]

We really like the comment regarding corporate citizenship made by Stephen W. Sanger, Chairman and CEO of General Mills. Consider what Sanger implies about the obligations of those of us who have skills and gifts honed in the business world:

> We believe we have a responsibility to reach out to others (outside the corporation), to take what we know and do what we can to make a difference. [It is wrong] to just work through the challenges of everyday business [and dismiss the] problems of the world—hunger, poverty, homelessness, illiteracy—[as] too vexing.[41]

Ramping Up with Stakeholder Connections

Companies always seek to distinguish themselves—through innovation of operational efficiency and offering new products, better quality, or value—but we believe that companies will increasingly be concerned as never before about their reputations for being not only ethical but generous.

We have shared the growing evidence that good corporate citizenship is good for business performance. As a result, more firms will envision corporate giving as an important part of their overall strategy and corporate culture, as illustrated by General Mills and others. If they choose to be involved in social activism as well, then firms will run the risk of alienating (or at least annoying) some stakeholders while gaining greater devotion from those sharing the same philosophy.

Corporate citizenship is one means of obtaining exponential power with the engagement of multiple stakeholders. Ethical business practices, corporate giving, consistent high-quality goods and services, confident senior management who develop and communicate a strategy with great clarity: These combined attributes energize individuals inside and outside the organization. A motivated workforce services customers better and performs well in volunteer work. Positive customers and opinion leaders in turn speak favorably of the company, which sparks the interest not only of other buyers, but of investors and media as well.

In Chapter 9 we explore these linkages between the effective management of different stakeholders and the compounding benefits for those companies that have managers who can achieve it.

The Power of Stakeholder Integration

In the previous chapter we discussed how corporate citizenship brings synergy between stakeholders and, ultimately, develops stronger commitment to the organization. Part of a leader's job is to clarify the mission and strategy of an organization and ensure that there is balance not only between the cost/productivity goals and the people (stakeholder) loyalty goals, but in the company's relationships with various stakeholders. As we strengthen relationships in a proportionate way with each stakeholder segment, those actions will create positive effects on our relationships with other segments and on the performance of the total enterprise as well.

To test this point in a minor way, just answer a question: Have you become more aware of or newly impressed with any of the companies highlighted in this book? If the answer is "yes," it proves the point that building exceptional relationships or otherwise meeting

stakeholders' needs has an impact on other (prospective) stakeholders.

There is a logical process to energizing stakeholders, beginning
with maintaining a compelling enough business model to be profitable. In that sense, markets (customers) and shareholders come
first. But as we establish value for customers and cash flow for owners, we must also recognize the crucial role that employees play in
the value chain. Employees are like the engine that carries a business
and its operation toward the destination of winning in the marketplace. And learning how to attract, energize, and keep the right people is the fuel for continued success. The point is that businesses
must manage to keep all of the components—compelling business
model, stock value, and energized employees—in balance.

Returning to the Power of Employees

We have pointed out already that in addition to helping the public
image side of corporate reputation, focusing on stakeholder relationships results in committed customers who give recommendations to
prospective customers and highly engaged employees who are much
more inclined to recruit other candidates to the firm. But perhaps the
most intriguing outcome of taking a stakeholder focus is the way the
commitment of employees helps to lift the commitment of customers.

Harvard Business Review published an article in the January/Feb-
ruary 1998 issue that has become a modern classic among human resource executives and organizational development professionals. The
article, "The Employee—Customer—Profit Chain at Sears," told how
CEO Arthur Martinez was making dramatic changes (including the
demise of the Sears catalog) to revive this once-proud firm that had
seen its customers migrate to Wal-Mart and the discount trade by the
1990s.[1] One of the changes Martinez introduced was an adaptation of
precepts from *The Service Profit Chain*, a book by J. L. Heskett, W. E.
Sasser, and L. A. Schlesinger.[2] This business model looks at a cause-and-
effect relationship that begins with management practices and is fol-

lowed by changes to employee attitudes, then to customer perceptions, and finally to the top-line financials. Through research, Sears
was able to quantify the effect of employee perceptions on customer
satisfaction and spending behavior at Sears. More specifically, the
company found that a 5 percentage point improvement in employee
attitudes drove a corresponding 1.3-point improvement in customer
satisfaction; the increased customer satisfaction in turn drove a 0.5-
point growth in store revenues. Figure 9.1 represents the employee-
customer-profit chain used by Sears.

By refocusing strategy and the organizational culture on these priorities, Sears at the time was able to achieve a remarkable recovery of
share and growth. (Now Sears has hit another slump, and Martinez is
taking new steps to climb out again. Retailing in the new world of e-
commerce as well as against the likes of Wal-Mart, Gap, and Home Depot is no cakewalk!) The legacy of this case, however, is in the proof
of employee impact on customers and, ultimately, on business performance.

Beyond its linkage with customer commitment, employee commitment as an outcome of worker motivation also directly affects financial performance. According to a study by E. R. Bashaw and S. E. Grant,
published in the *Journal of Personal Selling and Sales Management*
in 1994, committed employees are harder and more efficient workers
than less-committed workers, based on sales figures.[3]

The Watson Wyatt consulting firm recently confirmed that employees affect the bottom line with what they call a Human Capital Index,
constructed of corporate characteristics including recruiting excellence, clear rewards and accountability, a collegial and flexible workplace, communications integrity, and prudent use of resources. After
studying 405 U.S. publicly traded firms, each averaging 9,000 employees and $1.5 billion in annual revenue, they reported dramatically
greater returns to shareholders by the firms with higher human capital indices.[4]

We suggested earlier in the book that one could argue about
whether customers or employees are more important to a business.
Employees may never take precedence over customers in a debate,

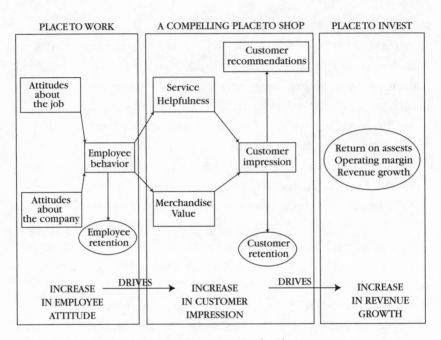

FIGURE 9.1   Sears' Employee-Customer-Profit Chain
Source:"The Employee—Customer—Profit Chain at Sears," *Harvard Business Review* (January/February 1998).

but studies such as the ones described previously tend to show time and again how crucial it is to work "from the inside out" in building stakeholder relationships. In other words, management must first build up its "human capital" to achieve its other goals. Workforce issues should be among a business's highest priorities for a variety of reasons discussed throughout this book: Talented people are becoming increasingly scarce; we are still working out the "new deal" of employment; and, as in the Sears profit chain example, the collaboration and support we want with customers, suppliers, and other outside stakeholders starts with the associates, our partners-on-the-inside who carry out those plans.

Thus, seeking dialogue and assessment from employees is critical if we are to know what they most care about related to their jobs and how best to attract and retain them. Some of the major dimensions on which to collect feedback about expectations include:

> *Fairness at work:* the perceived fairness of policies,
> compensation, performance review process, and hiring
> practices
> *Organizational learning:* the ability of the organization to
> innovate, teach, and be adaptive to market changes
> *Communication:* the flow and transparency of needed
> information
> *Flexibility and concern:* how employees are supported in
> their need for flexible schedules and work/life balancing
> *Customer focus:* consciousness of workforce and culture of
> the urgency and primacy of giving value to the customer
> *Trust and empowerment:* privacy, responsibility, decision
> making, and team involvement
> *Manager effectiveness/clarity of direction:* clear and
> effective direction, communication of strategy
> *Job satisfaction:* being adequately supported resource-wise,
> being put in the right roles, feeling valued

Getting feedback on these and other issues usually prompts additional dialogue and guides initiatives that help build the commitment level of employees over time. Given the "new deal" with workers, measuring just their loyalty to the larger organization may simply no longer be realistic. Instead, we must also find ways to help them develop stronger commitment to work teams or their local management.

The Stakeholder View at 30,000 Feet

Aside from singling out employee commitment as the conduit to all other stakeholders, we need to gain the "aerial view" of how various stakeholder groups interact. Most companies still manage various stakeholders in a fragmented way. For example, sales and customer service focus on customers, marketing deals with prospects, and communications talks with all other stakeholders. To work toward a system that manages multiple stakeholder groups and takes advantage of the impact that certain stakeholders have on others, we need a more holistic model of how stakeholders fit within the organization. The generic structure and flow in Figure 9.2 suggests a model that might work for many organizational structures.[5]

This model gives at least a starting framework for seeing various stakeholders within the company's broader chain of value and ultimate financial performance. Simply stated:

- Our guiding core values or principles and leadership philosophy create a culture that drives business practices and internal processes.
- The practices and processes in turn affect the perceptions not only of employees, but customers and other stakeholders as well.
- Employee behaviors directly affect customers and any other stakeholders they come into contact with.
- Employee productivity, customer repurchasing, as well as other stakeholders' behaviors directly affect the measures of business success.[6]

Another implication of seeing the larger picture of stakeholders in contact with our firms is the realization that we need an integrated system of stakeholder feedback and satisfaction measures. Companies have been particularly hesitant to conduct employee surveys. Yet, understanding the evolving needs of employees appears in many ways to be the linchpin to our ability to manage and measure multiple stakeholder groups.

Stakeholder Power Principles

If we want to leverage the power of stakeholders, we must recognize that people count more than performance; in fact, people are our

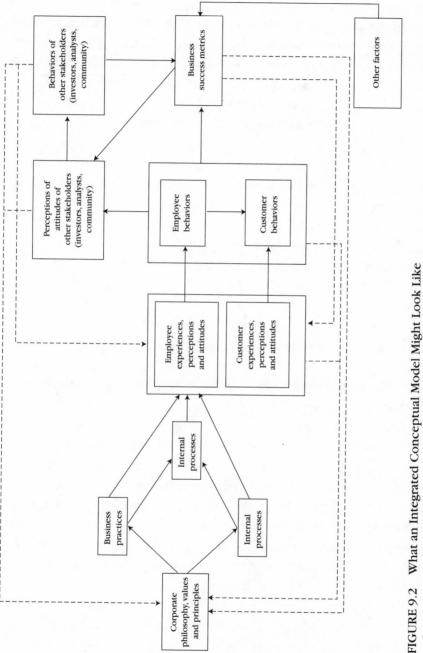

FIGURE 9.2 What an Integrated Conceptual Model Might Look Like

Source: Doug Grisaffe, "Understanding and Managing Linkages of Information Within Your Organization," presented at Walker Informational Global Network member training, Indianapolis, IN, June 22, 2000.

only means to the end. Although this precept has always been true in business, our accounting systems and perhaps human nature have led us to fixate on measuring and managing outcomes (financials, productivity, etc.) rather than focusing on the true leading indicators (employee commitment, customer loyalty, innovative business model design, etc.) in the new economy.

A white paper on metrics by the UK-based Metapraxis, an international business consultancy, asks, "Why do companies bother to collect and report information about the past when what they are trying to do is assist in the task of controlling the future?"[7] The way to control future business success is to be in close collaboration with the ones who will fulfill our strategies, which means we should be measuring and tracking their commitment as well.

We must make the effort to identify key stakeholder segments and a profile of

- how they will collaborate with our associates and
- tactics for moving them through the gates of loyalty.

In this effort, a simple matrix is useful to construct (see Table 9.1).

Arguably the biggest void within the new discipline of balanced performance measures has been the low caliber of people metrics. Business-to-business relationships require real dialogue with stakeholders and thorough assessments of relationships, rather than just customer servicing and purchasing histories or "report-card checks" following brief transactions. Of all the potentially powerful, predictive measures, the one most overlooked is the employee category. We delude ourselves unless we are tracking the commitment, concerns, and ideas of our workers. Leaders are most effective when they understand those whom they want to lead.

We cannot take for granted that people throughout our organizations in various locations (or even countries) are making ethical or even legal decisions every day. National employee surveys mentioned in Chapter 4 (not to mention human nature) say otherwise. And the risks are simply too high not to apply sound management practices to

TABLE 9.1 Gates of Loyalty Matrix

	Gate One—Awareness		Gate Two—Knowledge		Gate Three—Admiration		Gate Four—Action	
	Goals	Measures	Goals	Measures	Goals	Measures	Goals	Measures
Prospective Employees								
Employees								
Customers								
Prospects								
Investors								
Opinion Leaders								
Regulators								
Others (list)								

business ethics. Corporate reputations are typically built over years, and with sweat and tears; but they can be lost overnight by one unethical act. The management of ethics begins with leaders clarifying and living the corporate values; larger organizations also require dedicated resources, such as codes of ethics, supervisor training, and reporting helplines.

Remember that building a dynamic business with stakeholder power principles means we must follow the hierarchy of stakeholder requirements. Like building blocks, fulfilling the next requirement is secured by having a more foundational one in place:

1. Create or maintain a compelling business model that offers a unique product or service value (desired price, service, features, etc.).
2. Sustain the business model with innovation and maintain an internal environment that will attract and keep talented employees.
3. Operate within legal and ethical boundaries, not only preserving corporate reputation but also impressing people and building self-respect.
4. Reach out to outside stakeholders, not only transparently informing them about your business but also finding worthy causes to support.

Every company should find its best-fit social outreach opportunity and commit to it for an extended period of time. The benefits will come back to us not only because, as the saying goes, "We reap what we sow," but because the journey itself will energize stakeholders both inside and outside our organization—not to mention those who are being helped, treated, or cared for.

Recognize in advance that this is not the easiest way to run a business—but it's the best and most rewarding way in the long run. For any large organization, the transition to stakeholder-based management will be difficult. Just maintaining balance between short-term financial objectives and future ones such as employee loyalty is very hard. Board members, owners, or shareholders will usually pressure leaders for immediate financial outcomes, despite evidence that stakeholder management creates the groundwork for future success. Our advice is to push back against those pressures. Use evidence from your own experience and from the studies shared in this book to argue your vision and take a stand for building stakeholder relationships.

At the same time, good balance requires keeping an unwavering eye on the foundation for building relationships, which is maintaining a competitive business model that offers customer value and can be operated profitably. So we can never forget innovation, marketing, and cost management, or, in the end, both the stockholder as well as the stakeholder will be hurt.

Two business cases follow that we believe represent very different approaches in this realm of balancing the stakeholder mission with the business mission.

• •

Case in Point: Levi Strauss & Company—
Can Corporate Citizenship Trump Market Appeal?

American culture owes much to San Francisco–based Levi Strauss and Company. Over a century ago, the company invented the waist-high overalls that eventually became known first as blue jeans and then just "jeans." Jeans became the uniform for outdoor working men in the United States, but the biggest turning point for the company was in the 1950s, when jeans became the official uniform for rebellious youth. By the 1960s, there were jeans styles for women and expansion overseas, and the baby-boomers kept on buying jeans through their college years and into their thirties.

But by the mid-1980s profits had declined due to changing styles, demographics (baby-boomers now wearing chinos, if not suits), and increased competition. It was at that time, according to Hoovers Online, that "Peace Corps Veteran–turned–McKinsey consultant" Robert Haas, a fifth-generation Strauss family member, took control of the company; within a year, he took the company semi-private after it had been publicly traded for 13 years. Haas took difficult steps in 1984 to keep the ship afloat—closing plants, selling subsidiaries, expanding overseas and renewing the company's focus on core products—and Levi's stock rose dramatically within a year's time.

But Haas apparently saw the righting of the business as just a first step toward a broader mission. Haas recalls that people at Levi's were unsure at the time what the company stood for; as leader, he provided the answer. "I said, let's fix the business first, but as soon as we have our business back on track we have to attend to our culture, because that's the glue that unites us, the beacon that guides our actions."[8] The company actually had a socially responsible heritage already. Since the 1960s, Levi Strauss employees had been encouraged to get involved in community support projects. The company pioneered "Community Involvement Teams" (CIFs), a concept for which it was recognized by the White House in 1984 with the President's Volunteer Action Award for Corporate Volunteerism. But wanting to do even more, Haas engineered what Hoovers describes as "a touchy-feely culture often at odds with the bottom line."[9] *Fortune* went further in an April 1999 article, calling the company "a failed utopian management experiment." Haas believed in giving the rank-and-file workers at Levi's a voice in major decisions, so there were many meetings—and many were often too lengthy or of questionable value. Robert Siegel, who left Levi's in 1993 to head up Stride Rite, was quoted as saying, "About half my time was spent in meetings that were absolutely senseless."[10]

Haas was absolutely committed to people at Levi's becoming "aspirational." Levi's Mission and Aspirations statement was literally printed on denim and posted prominently in all locations, including tenets of teamwork, trust, diversity, and empowerment. One-third of executives' bonuses was based on their managing "aspirationally," and 80 task forces were created to move the company to be the same. The core curriculum of company training in the early 1990s was a three-part, 10-day course focused on the mission and aspirations. During the course work, employee groups were asked to become very transparent in opening up about their personal fears and accomplishments. Haas himself at one time handed out AIDS pamphlets outside the corporate cafeteria and delivered outside speeches about the unique social mission and culture of the firm.[11]

There is no question that some people were helped by the social activities of Levi's during this time, and many employees stayed fiercely loyal to the company, its mission, and its culture. However, if all the changes to the culture were not downright harmful to Levi's business performance, then they were at the very least a distraction, because the company clearly lost sight of emerging competitive threats, demands by retailers, and trends in the consumer marketplace. And the "principled reasoning" approach to making decisions at Levi's made the company ill-equipped to change direction or revise operational processes quickly.[12]

Despite the success of its Dockers casual pants (introduced in 1986), Levi Strauss had hit hard times again by the mid-1990s, largely because the children of baby-boomers were buying brands other than the Levi's product and in many cases weren't even shopping in stores carrying the Levi's brand. Like the youth of a prior generation, the fashion sense of these young people was intentionally completely different from their parents—in this case, wanting much bigger, over-sized, wide-legged jeans and pants. In the meantime, even the parents' tastes were changing. Not only were aging baby-boomers questioning whether they could still look good in jeans, but many were less than impressed by the image-laden ads of Levi Strauss. Market share for Levi Strauss, which was still at 30 percent or so at the beginning of the 1990s, had been cut nearly in half by 2000; the result was cutting jobs and closing factories again, especially in the United States. In September 1999, Haas turned over the CEO position to Pepsi executive Phillip Marineau, with an ensuing restructuring of company management.[13]

Levi Strauss forgot the mandate that great social responsibility can only be sustained in a competitive marketplace when the business maintains high customer value. As recently retired Levi's President Peter Jacobi put it, "the problem is that some people thought the values were an end in themselves." And *Fortune* drew a similar conclusion: "Levi's wasn't just a garment company committed to so-cial responsibility. It was a politically correct organization that hap-pened to be in the garment business."[14]

. . . .

Case in Point: LensCrafters— Packaging Value for Customers, Purpose for Employees, and Missions for Communities

The tale of LensCrafters represents one of the great success stories in retailing. The company has been financially successful to be sure, but equally effective in other important ways that exemplify some of the points we have tried to make in this book

The company didn't exist until 1983, and began on the strength of a unique business model. In a business category traditionally dominated by local eyeglass stores and eye care professionals, this upstart firm began bringing together in the same location the eye doctor, lens-grinding laboratory, and a broad selection of eyeglass frames, enabling the delivery of eyeglasses in about a hour. Such a breakthrough in one-stop shopping and customer convenience fu-eled its growth. The stores, typically located in or near shopping malls so people could shop during the time they waited to pick up their new eyewear, were by 1986 being added at a rate of two stores per week. By 1989, LensCrafters totaled 363 stores and had become America's largest chain of optical superstores.[15]

In the 1990s, under the leadership of then-CEO Dave Browne, the corporate strategy shifted. Growth continued at a more controlled rate, as did emphasis on the quality of in-store service and eyewear selection. But the company really began concentrating on improving efficiency and productivity. One major step was installing an entirely new labor management system called SMART (Store Management and Associates at the Right Time). This automated system enhanced the optimal scheduling of associates, forecasting labor needs based on customer traffic, budget, and labor forecasts by store location. Such a system was particularly needed at LensCrafters, given the complexity of having retail/lab/affiliated optometrists in the same of-fice environment. This new system exemplified the company's commitment to "constantly, measurably improve."[16] But achieving greater efficiency of personnel and bottom-line improvement for shareholders was balanced at the time by better understanding the ongoing needs of customers and of workers as well.

To address customer needs beyond the convenience of one-stop shopping, LensCrafters added customer value in other ways: showing price tags on eyewear to aid comparison shopping; changing eye-frame styles and selection in keeping with customer tastes; and developing innovative lens technology such as the new progressive lens with 25 percent wider viewing area, designed especially for the aging baby-boomer market.[17]

To ensure that it was meeting the changing expectations of customers, LensCrafters had initiated by the early 1990s a continuous, sophisticated customer feedback program reporting customer in-store service commitment scores on a quarterly basis down to a region and even a per-store basis. A portion of management incentives is based on meeting goals set to improve customer rating scores. Top-performing store managers are asked to share their approaches to customer relationships with the rest of the operation. The program has definitely helped the company track changing customer expectations and guide store-level procedures and employee training resources that ultimately make customers feel that they want to return to LensCrafters.

Earning the commitment of employees at LensCrafters started with helping them understand the broader vision of the firm: "helping the world to see." Retail associates were to be "vision care specialists." To anchor the degree to which they value their associates, leadership strived to develop LensCrafters into one of the world's most appealing places to work. Over the years, the company has regularly surveyed employees and responded to their changing needs by offering flextime, discounts at childcare centers, an elder care program, compressed work weeks, and a 401(k) program in which the company matches each $1 employee contribution with $1.50. Workers also appreciate receiving their own 50 percent discount on eyewear.

By astutely monitoring the quality of employee relationships, LensCrafters created loyalty in the workforce to a degree that most managers would envy. Independent surveys rank LensCrafters among the top 5 to 10 percent of all firms in employee satisfaction. In 1999, the editors of *Fortune* placed LensCrafters once again on its coveted list, the "100 Best Companies to Work for in America"; and the company moved notably higher on the list, within the top 50 for 2000.[18]

But the unique attraction of the LensCrafters culture cannot be understood without knowing about its unique sense of mission. As a part of the company's "Give the Gift of Sight" program, employees collect, regrind, and give away eyeglasses to the poor—more than 1 million pairs to date in countries around the world. Employees speak with justifiable pride about this program and consider it a privilege to participate on "mission trips," in which trained volunteers conduct temporary clinics that are set up to fit local children and adults with the eyeglasses they need. These international missions are conducted in partnership with Lions Clubs International. Domestic volunteer programs include the LensCrafters Vision Van, which conducts exams and fits eyewear for residents in locations ranging from inner-city New York to Fall River Indian Reservation in Nevada. On Hometown Day, all LensCrafters stores open early so that the needy in those communities can receive free eye exams and eye glasses.

The Gift of Sight program did not begin as a business strategy, but rather as a good way for the company to help its local communities. Yet its impact on employees has been broad and deep. All 17,000 or so employees have participated. Cliff Bartow, chief operating officer of LensCrafters, said of the program that when it began in 1988, "we knew we'd change the lives of the recipients. Twelve years later, we can't tell who benefits the most—those who give the gift of sight or those who receive it." [19]

So the LensCrafters story is one of success built around a distinctive business model that offers customer value combined with corporate values that give employees a sense of purpose. Upon that foundation, associates have been further inspired, working in an environment sensitive to their needs and feeling they are a business that truly makes a difference in the lives of individuals.

A November 2000 *Chicago Tribune* article about philanthropy provided testimony from Naomi Rodriguez, general manager of a LensCrafters store in Merrillville, Indiana, regarding her attraction to this employer:

The salary was the same (in my prior job at the time that LensCrafters recruited me), so why should I go? What truly inspired me to accept was the company's free eyeglasses for people who can't afford them. And what makes me want to stay is our Gift of Sight program in which employees go as volunteers throughout the United States and to foreign countries to give eye exams and provide glasses to the underprivileged.[20]

Rodriguez, at the time of the article, had already traveled on Gift of Sight missions to Bolivia and Jamaica. She had also joined the Vision Van mobile unit on a trip throughout the Chicago area that treated children and adult residents. Rodriguez, who earned a degree in organizational management and manages a staff of 35, said, "Companies that don't give back to their communities are missing an important connection with their employees."[21]

The unique culture at LensCrafters has been noticed by outsiders as well. Consider this testimony from a stakeholder on the outside, Joe Calloway, a customer of LensCrafters but also a business speaker and writer who works with them on occasion:

My experience as a customer of LensCrafters is that they not only want to sell me new glasses, they want me to love my new glasses. My (inside) experience with LensCrafters as a business speaker is that their meetings are 90% about the joy of helping people see better. They get their greatest fulfillment from their work overseas providing eyeglasses at no charge to people who could otherwise never have them. It's who they are. And this sense of purpose carries over into their stores. You know:

1) Who LensCrafters is [Awareness Gate];
2) What they promise [Knowledge Gate]; and
3) That they keep the promise [Admiration Gate]. [References to the gates of loyalty are ours.][22]

This explains in his own words how Joe Calloway has been taken step-by-step up to and through the fourth and highest gate of loyalty—Action—becoming a customer and consultant who now gives LensCrafters testimonials. Now that is stakeholder power!

LensCrafters' success shows the power of measuring and managing relationships continuously to reinforce the need for commitment, not just from employees, but from customers as well. Employees who comply with the dictates of their jobs deliver competent performance. But the company also counts on employees like Naomi Rodriguez, who are not only competent but excited. Being emotionally and behaviorally committed to their company, they are then willing to recruit prospective workers and deliver performance that customers cannot resist.

Companies well grounded in their market focus and ethical practices have, in a sense, earned the right to do good. With effective corporate giving, companies receive a bonus: a "tiebreaker" reputation attribute that will prove alluring to many prospective employees and other stakeholders. A study of 1,000 Americans by Cone Inc., a Boston-based consulting firm, indicates that about three in four (76 percent) would select the firm supporting a cause when offered two positions of otherwise similar pay and responsibility.[23] As Mark A. Feldman, Cone Inc., Executive Vice President, puts it: "Employees are searching for a company that they are proud to be a part of—not only because of the work that is accomplished, but also because of what the company stands for."[24]

• •

We must commit ourselves to "wrestling" with this stakeholder stuff! It will not be as easy as operating with a very narrow or short-term focus, but the rewards are greater and more meaningful. Only a brave leader explores what the troops really think. And as business leaders, we live in a world of immediacy, with quarterly financial reports seeming to come as fast as if they were monthly ones. But to be a true leader in the new economy, we must earn the trust of all our key stakeholders by learning to place faith in people and by weighing their needs and opinions into our business decisions. If we as managers use tools to listen to them, then collaborate with them fairly and intelligently, we will take care of the business and its constituents and, as a result, take care of ourselves as well.

Notes

Chapter One

1. Robert Lenzner and Stephen S. Johnson, "Seeing Things As They Really Are," *Forbes Magazine* (March 10, 1997); http://www.forbes.com/forbes/97/0310/5905122a.htm (June 22, 2000). Drucker, the subject of this article, lent his insight into the future of business and education in the United States.

2. Lester C. Thurow, "Building Wealth," *The Atlantic Monthly* (June 1999); http://www.theatlantic.com/issues/99jun/9906thurow.htm (June 27, 2000).

3. Ignazio Visco, "The New Economy: Fact or Fiction?" *OECD Observer* (June 27, 2000); http://www.oecdobserver.org/news/fullstory.php3/aid/270 (July 5, 2000).

4. Timothy Aeppel and Clare Ansberry, "Eaton Chairman Says Old Industry Matters, Though Game Has Changed," *The Wall Street Journal Interactive Edition* (June 22, 2000); http://interactive.wsj.com/ushome.html (June 22, 2000).

5. "Is Work Bad for You?" *The Atlantic Monthly* (June 2000); http://www.theatlantic.com/issues/99aug/9908badwork.htm (June 27, 2000).

6. Louis Csoka, "Introduction," in *The New Deal in Employment Relationships: A Council Report,* ed. Brian Hackett (New York: Conference Board, 1996), 5.

7. Cliff Hakim, "Building Conscious Loyalty," in *The New Deal in Employment Relationships: A Council Report,* ed. Brian Hackett (New York: Conference Board, 1996), 19–24.

233

8. "The 100 Best Companies to Work For," *Fortune* 141, no. 1 (January 10, 2000): 2-4.

9. Katie Sosnowchik, "Do-It-Yourself Green," *Green@work Magazine* (March/April 2000): 16.

10. "Defining 'Sustainability'," *Green@work Magazine* (March/April 2000): 26.

11. "What Is OECD," *OECD home page,* http://www.oecd.org/about/general/index.htm (July 5, 2000).

Chapter Two

1. Walker Information, sponsor, "1998 North American Study on Stakeholder Measurement," *Measurements* 8, no. 3; www.walkerinfo.com.

2. Milton Friedman, *Capitalism and Freedom* (Chicago: University of Chicago Press, 1963), 133.

3. Terrence E. Deal and Allan A. Kennedy, *The New Corporate Cultures* (Reading, Mass.: Perseus Books, 1999), 44-45.

4. Ibid., 44.

5. Ibid., 49.

6. Ibid., 52.

7. Bill Birchard, "How Many Masters Can You Serve?" *CFO Magazine* (July 1995): 48-54.

8. John A. Byrne, "The Shredder," *BusinessWeek* (January 15, 1996); http://www.businessweek.com/1996/03/b34581.htm (August 2000).

9. John A. Byrne, *Chainsaw: The Notorious Career of Al Dunlap in the Era of Profit-at-Any-Price* (New York: Harper Business, 1999).

10. Dwight L. Gertz and Joao P.A. Baptista, *Grow to Be Great* (New York: Free Press, 1995), 7-21.

11. Michael Rion, *The Responsible Manager* (Amherst, Mass.: Human Resource Development Press, 1986), 50-51.

12. Birchard, "How Many Masters Can You Serve?," 48-54.

13. Ibid.

14. Ibid.

15. Ibid.

16. John P. Kotter, and James L. Heskett, *Corporate Culture and Performance* (New York: Free Press, 1992).

17. James C. Collins and Jerry I. Porras, *Built to Last* (New York: Harper Business School Press, 1994).

18. Ibid., 45.

19. Jonathan Low, and Tony Siesfield, "Measures That Matter: Non-financial Performance," *Strategy and Leadership* 26, no. 2 (March/April 1998); http://www.pbviews.com/magazine/articles/measures_that_matter.html.

20. "America's Most Admired Companies," *Fortune* (July 13, 2000; http://www.fortune.com/fortune/mostadmired/gat.html (July 31, 2000).

21. Jeff Frooman, "Socially Irresponsible and Illegal Behavior and Shareholder Wealth," *Business and Society Review* 36 (September 1997): 221.

22. David Weldon, "Best Places to Work in IT 2000," *Computerworld* (July 3, 2000); http://www.computerworld.com/cwi/story/0,1199,NAV47_STO45408,00.html (July 31, 2000).

23. Amy Bryer, "Lockheed Tries to Overcome Setbacks," *The Denver Business Journal* (April 17, 2000); http://www.bizjournals.com/denver/stories/2000/04/17/story7.html (July 28, 2000).

24. Jeremy Hope, and Tony Hope, *Competing in the Third Wave* (Boston: Harvard Business School Press, 1997), 172.

25. Private Securities Reform Act 1995, H.R. 1058, ENR Sec. 102, 'SEC 27A.

26. Low and Siesfield, "Measures That Matter: Non-financial Performance."

27. Alan M. Webber, "New Math for a New Economy," *Fast Company* (January/February 2000); http://www.fastcompany.com/online/31/lev.html (August 31, 2000).

28. Quoted in ibid.

29. Jeremy Hope and Tony Hope, *Competing in the Third Wave* (Boston: Harvard Business School Press, 1997), 171.

30. Ibid., 172.

31. Quoted in Webber, "New Math for a New Economy."

32. Robert S. Kaplan and David P. Norton, *The Balanced Scorecard* (Boston: Harvard Business School Press, 1996), 22-23.

33. "Ethics and Social Accountability," British Telecommunications White Paper, http://www.bt.com/World/environment/bal/ethical.htm (August 1, 2000).

34. "BT's Social Report 1999: Shareholder," http://62.172.196.103/World/society/rep99/ (August 1, 2000).

35. Ibid.

Chapter Three

1. Douglas J. Edwards, "The Best 100," *IndustryWeek* (August 16, 1999); http://www.industryweek.com/iwinprint/BestManaged/1999/database/iw1000names99.asp (July 19, 2000).

2. Foundation for the Malcolm Baldrige National Quality Award, "The Nation's CEOs Look to the Future," July 1998, http://www.quality.nist.gov/ceo-rpt.htm (August 10, 2000).

3. Baldrige National Quality Program, *2000 Criteria for Performance Excellence* (Gaithersburg, MD: National Institute of Standards and Technology, 2000).

4. Frederick F. Reichheld, *The Loyalty Effect* (Boston: Harvard Business School Press, 1996).

5. John P. Meyer and Natalie J. Allen, *Commitment in the Workplace* (London: Sage Publications, 1997), 11–12.

6. Allen S. Dick and Kunal Basu, "Customer Loyalty: Toward an Integrated Conceptual Framework," *Journal of the Academy of Marketing Science* 22, no. 2 (Spring 1994): 100.

7. Tom Wailgum, "Loyalty Complex," *CIO Magazine* (May 1, 2000); http://www.cio.com/archive/050100_reality_content.html (August 11, 2000).

8. *Inside CDW web page.* http://www.cdw.com/webcontent/inside/inside/default.asp. (10 August 2000).

9. "CDW Computer Centers," *Urban Tapestry Series: Profiles,* http://www.urbantapestry.com/chicago/profiles/profile80.htm (February 2001).

Chapter Four

1. Stephen Carter, "The Insufficiency of Honesty," *Atlantic Monthly* (February 1996): 74.

2. Jeff Frooman, "Socially Irresponsible and Illegal Behavior and Shareholder Wealth," *Business and Society* 36 (September 1997): 221.

3. "Quick Q&A's," Social Investment Forum website, http://www.socialinvest.org/Areas/news/index.html.

4. "Socially Responsible Mutual Fund Performance," *Business Ethics* 14 (January/February 2000): 28.

5. Walker Information, sponsor, "1994 Study on Corporate Character," www.walkerinfo.com.

6. Ann Svendsen, *The Stakeholder Strategy* (San Francisco: Berrett-Koehler Publishers, 1998).

7. *KPMG Report on Organizational Integrity* (Washington, DC: KPMG Integrity Management, Risk Advisors Services, 2001).

8. Walker Information and Hudson Institute, sponsors, "1999 Employee Retention and Business Integrity Study," www.walkerinfo.com.

9. *KPMG Report.*

10. Carter,"The Insufficiency of Honesty."

11. James C. Collins and Jerry I. Porras, *Built to Last* (New York: Harper Business, 1994), 1.

12. Des Dearlove and Stephen J. Coomber, "Heart and Soul" (May 1999), www.blessingwhite.com.

13. Michael Gropp, personal communication with author Jeff Marr, September 1998.

14. Debbie LeClair, O. C. Ferrell, and John Fraedrich, *Integrity Management* (Tampa: University of Tampa Press, 1998).

15. American Society of Chartered Life Underwriters & Chartered Financial Consultants and Ethics Office Association, *Sources and Consequences of Workplace Pressure* (Bryn Mawr, PA: American Society of CLU & ChFC, 1997).

16. Collins, and Porras, *Built to Last.*

17. LeClair, Ferrell, and Fraedrich, *Integrity Management,* 39.

18. Michael Rion, *The Responsible Manager* (Amherst, Mass: Human Resource Development Press, 1986), 23.

19. Rion, *The Responsible Manager,* 13–14.

20. Walker Information,"1997 Business Integrity Study."

21. Dawn-Marie Driscoll and Michael Hoffman, *Ethics Matters* (Waltham, Mass.: Bentley College, 2000), 13–14.

22. Victoria Wesseler, personal communication with author Jeff Marr, March 8, 2001.

23. Walker Information and Hudson Institute, sponsors, "1999 National Business Ethics Study," www.walkerinfo.com.

24. *KPMG Report.*

25. "100 Best Companies to Work For," *Fortune* (January 10, 2000): front cover.

26. "Managing Ethics in Today's Changing Utility Industry," Sears Lectureship in Business Ethics, Bentley College, Waltham, Massachusetts, November 2, 1999.

27. Driscoll and Hoffman, *Ethics Matters,* 10.

Chapter Five

1. Walker Information, sponsor, "1999 International Stakeholder Study," www.walkerinfo.com.

2. "Malcolm Baldrige National Quality Award 1989 Winner," http://www.quality.nist.gov/winners/xerox.htm (August 16, 2000).

3. Benjamin Gomes-Casseres, "The Competing in Constellations: The Case of Fuji Xerox," First Quarter 1997, http://www.strategy-business.com/case-study/97108/page1.html (August 8, 2000).

4. Walker Information Global Network, "A Compilation of 84 Individual Client Studies across Industries," 2000 data.

5. *Jiffy Lube Company Information home page*, http://www.jiffylube.com/company/default.asp (August 8, 2000).

6. Hoovers Online, "NCR Corporation Profile," http://www.hoovers.com (November 15, 2000).

7. "Press Release of announcement of 1998 National Builder of the Year award by *Professional Builder Magazine*," http://www.centexhomes.com/pb.htm (November 2000).

8. David Sasina, Senior Vice President—Marketing, Centex Corporation, personal communication with Walker Information associates, November 2000.

9. Ibid.

10. "America's Most Admired Firms," *Fortune* (February 21, 2000): 108–16.

11. Stephen J. Wall and Shannon Rye Wall, *The Morning After* (Cambridge, MA: Perseus Publishing, 2000), 27.

12. *NCR Corporate Fact Sheet home page*, http://www3.ncr.com/fact_sheet.html (August 17, 2000).

13. Client contacts on the NCR project, personal communication with Walker Information associates, Fall 1999.

Chapter Six

1. Quoted in Robert Lenzner and Stephen S. Johnson, "Seeing Things as They Really Are," *Forbes* (March 10, 1997); http://www.forbes.com/forbes/97/0310/5905122a.htm (June 2000).

2. Dwight L. Gertz and João P. A. Baptista, *Grow to Be Great* (New York: The Free Press, 1995), 37.

3. Terrence E. Deal and Allan A. Kennedy, *The New Corporate Cultures* (Cambridge, MA: Perseus Publishing, 1999), 77.

4. Ibid.

5. Walker Information and Hudson Institute, sponsors, "1999 Employee Retention and Business Integrity Study," www.walkerinfo.com.

6. Cliff Hakim, "Building Conscious Loyalty," in *The New Deal in Employment Relationships: A Council Report,* ed. Brian Hackett (New York: Conference Board, 1996), 19–24.

7. Patricia Milligan, "Regaining Commitment," in *The New Deal in Employment Relationships: A Council Report,* ed. Brian Hackett (New York: Conference Board, 1996), 8–11.

8. James P. Kelly, "The Loyalty Contract: Employee Commitment and Competitive Advantage," *UPS Pressroom home page,* http://pressroom.ups.com/execforum/speeches/viewspeech/0,1262,73,FF.html (March 28, 1998), 3.

9. Ibid., 1.

10. Ibid., 3–4.

11. "About UPS/Company History," http://www.pressroom.ups.com/about/history (March 28, 1998).

12. Kelly, "Loyalty Contract" (March 28, 1998).

13. Ibid.

14. Ibid.

15. Foundation for the Malcolm Baldrige National Quality Award, "The Nation's CEOs Look to the Future," July 1998, http://www.quality.nist.gov/ceorpt.htm (December 1999).

16. "Standardized Unemployment Rates" (news release, April 6, 2000), *OECD Online,* http://www.oecd.org/media/new_numbers/sur/nw00-29a.htm (August 14, 2000).

17. The Bureau of National Affairs, Inc., "Economy Spurs Highest Turnover Rates in Nearly 20 Years, BNA Survey Finds" (press release, September 24, 1998), http://www.bna.com/press/pr00.htm (March 13, 2000).

18. Bureau of Labor Statistics, "Labor Force Statistics from the Current Population Survey," http://stats.bls.gov/newsrels.htm.

19. Richard W. Judy and Carol D'Amico, *Workforce 2020: Work and Worker in the 21st Century* (Indianapolis: Hudson Institute, 1998).

20. Ibid., 78–81.

21. Deborah Austin, "Growing Companies Report," *IndustryWeek* (July 19, 2000); http://www.industryweek.com/iwgc/newsbriefs.asp.

22. Ibid.

23. Robert Levering and Milton Moskowitz, "The 100 Best Companies to Work For," *Fortune* (January 10, 2000): 82–110.

24. "Labours Lost," *The Economist* (July 15, 2000); http://www.economist.com/PrinterFriendly.cfm?Story_ID=5988.

25. Ibid.

26. From a "Turnover Cost Worksheet," courtesy of Integrated Organizational Development, Hudson Institute, and Walker Information, 2000.

27. Walker Information and Hudson Institute, "1999 Employee Retention and Business Integrity Study."

28. J. Lingle and W. Schiemann, "From Balanced Scorecard to Strategic Gauges: Is Measurement Worth It?" *Management Review* (March 1996): 56–61.

29. Joe Folkman and Jack Zenger, *Employee Surveys That Make a Difference* (Provo, UT: Executive Excellence Publishing, 1999), 11.

30. Mike Foti, "Establishing a Vision Helps Build Loyalty Among Workers," *bizjournals.com website,* July 10, 2000, http://www.bizjournals.com/columbus/stories/2000/07/10/smallb3.html.

31. Quoted in George Donnelly, "Recruiting, Retention & Returns," *CFO* (March 2000): 68–76.

32. Ibid.

33. Ron St. Clair, President of Stalcop, personal communications with members of the Stalcop account team at Walker Information, November 2000.

34. Ibid.

35. Ibid.

36. Ibid.

37. Ibid.

38. Ibid.

39. Douglas Grisaffe, paper submitted and being reviewed for publication in the *Journal of Customer Satisfaction/Dissatisfaction and Complaining Behavior*.

40. Ron St. Clair, personal communication with staff at Walker Information, June 2000.

Chapter Seven

1. "Why Networking?," *Monster.com: Career Management,* http://content.monster.com/career/networking/bigdeal (December 5, 2000).

2. Walker Information and Hudson Institute, sponsors, "1999 National Business Ethics Study," www.walkerinfo.com.

3. James F. Moore, *The Death of Competition* New York: HarperBusiness, 1996).

4. Ibid., 54.

5. Allan A. Kennedy, *The End of Shareholder Value* Cambridge, MA: Perseus Publishing, 2000).

6. Ibid., 135.

7. Ibid., 140.

8. Charles Fombrun, *Reputation: Realizing Value from the Corporate Image* (Boston: Harvard Business School Press, 1996).

9. *The Wall Street Journal Interactive Edition, Wsj.com website,* http://interactive.wsj.com.

10. 1994 Walker Corporate Character Study; available upon request at www.wwalkerinfo.com. This was a study of 1,037 heads of households, asking about the social responsibility they expected of corporations.

11. Todd Saxton, "The Effects of Partner and Relationship Characteristics on Alliance Outcomes," *Academy of Management Journal* 40, no. 2 (April 1997): 443–461.

12. Hill & Knowlton and *Chief Executive Magazine* "Survey of Chief Executive Officers," http://www.hillandknowlton.com/corp_survey.asp.

13. Ibid.

14. Seth Sutel, "Hoax Sends Tech Stock Plunging," *Yahoo! News website,* August 25, 2000, http://dailynews.yahoo.com/h/ap/20000825/bs/stock_plunge_hoax_3.html.

15. Ibid.

16. Ibid.

17. Hill & Knowlton and *Chief Executive Magazine,* "Survey of Chief Executive Officers."

18. Walker Information account staff, personal communications with Edison International staff, March–May 1998.

Chapter Eight

1. Archie B. Carroll, "The Pyramid of Corporate Social Responsibility: Toward the Moral Management of Organizational Stakeholders," *Business Horizons* (July-August 1991): 39.

2. M. N. Vamos, "America—Land of the Shaken," *BusinessWeek* (March 11, 1996): 64–65.

3. Peyback Classic Advertisement, *Indianapolis Star,* August 25, 2000.

4. Council on Foundations, *Measuring the Value of Corporate Citizenship* (Washington, DC: Council on Foundations, Inc., 1996), v.

5. Karl Taro Greenfield, "A New Way of Giving," *Time* (July 24, 2000): 48–59.

6. Michael A. Verespej, "Why They're the Best," *IndustryWeek* (August 16, 2000); http://industryweek.com/CurrentArticles/asp/articles.asp?ArticleID=592.

7. Greenfield, "A New Way of Giving."

8. Ibid., 51.

9. "The 1999 Cone/Roper Cause Related Trends Report," presented at the Special Olympics Marketing Conference, Arlington, VA, May 2, 2000.

10. The Fund Raising School, "1997 Report of Philanthropic Giving," *Giving USA* from *The Chronicle of Philanthropy* (1999).

11. *Council on Foundations website,* http://www.cof.org/membersonly/NewWindowView.cfm?path=/membersonly/membershipinfo/1998stats/AssetsGrants/AssetsGrants.htm.

12. "The 1999 Cone/Roper Cause Related Trends Report."

13. Council on Foundations, *Measuring the Value of Corporate Citizenship*.

14. Greenfield, "A New Way of Giving."

15. Ibid.

16. "Measuring the Business Value of Corporate Philanthropy," Research Report by Walker Information, October 2000. Available at *Council on Foundations website,* http://www.cof.org.

17. "The 1999 Cone/Roper Cause Related Trends Report."

18. Ibid.

19. "Measuring the Business Value of Corporate Philanthropy."

20. Ibid.

21. "Basic Facts About United Way," *United Way website,* http://national.unitedway.org/bfact.htm.

22. Ibid.

23. Nye Lavalle & Associates, "The Charities Americans Like Most—and Least," *The Chronicle of Philanthropy* (December 13, 1996).

24. Sargent Shriver, "What's So Special about Special Olympics?" (background information for corporate sponsors), Special Olympics Marketing Conference, Arlington, Virginia, May 2, 2000.

25. Ibid.

26. "Employee Involvement—TEAM Advantage," presented by Kathy Mejasich at the Special Olympics Marketing Conference, Arlington, VA, May 2, 2000.

27. Ernest Beck and Shelley Branch, "Unilever Buys Ben & Jerry's, Slimfast for over $2.5 Billion," *Wall Street Journal Interactive Edition,* April 13, 2000; http://www.fbresearch.org/bodyshop.html.

28. Ben Cohen and Jerry Greenfield, *Ben & Jerry's Double-Dip* (New York: Simon & Schuster, 1997).

29. Beck and Branch, "Unilever Buys Ben & Jerry's."

30. Robert Tomsho, "Ben & Jerry's Founders May Quit Unilever Unit," *Wall Street Journal Interactive Edition,* November 21, 2000; htp://interactive.wsj.com/retrieve.cgi?id=SB974764554184917574.djm&te mplate=doclink.temp (december 11, 2000-.

31. http://www.savebenandjerry's.com.

32. Tamsho, "Ben & Jerry's Founders May Quit Unilever Unit."

33. Reuters Company News, "Consumer Group to Boycott Unilever Products," December 6, 2000.

34. Foundation for Biomedical Research, Animal Research facts, "1994 Article Challenges Ethical Image of the Body Shop," http://www.fbresearch.org.

35. Verespej, "Why They're the Best."

36. Press release, "General Mills Foundation Awards Grants," *General Mills website,* April 14, 1999, http://www.generalmills.com/news/releases/index.asp?newstype=2&storyID=472.

37. Verespej, "Why They're the Best."

38. Press release, "General Mills Assists Fire Fighters and Victims in New Mexico," *General Mills website,* May 11, 2000, http://www.generalmills.com/news/releases/index.asp?newstype=2&storyID=475.

39. Verespej, "Why They're the Best."

40. Minnesota Council on Foundations news archives, "General Mills, IBM, U S West Recognized for Corporate Leadership," *MCF website,* http://www.mcf.org/mcf/whatsnew/archives/June2000/rbrown000606.ht m.

41. Quoted in Verespej, "Why They're the Best."

Chapter Nine

1. Anthony J. Rucci, Steven P. Kirn, and Richard T. Quinn, "The Employee-Customer-Profit Chain at Sears," *Harvard Business Review* (January–February 1998); ttp://www.hbsp.harvard.edu/products/hbr/janfeb98/98109.html.

2. James L. Heskett, W. Earl Sassner, and Leonard A. Schlesinger, *The Service Profit Chain: How Leading Companies Link Profit and Growth to Loyalty, Satisfaction, and Value* (Westwood, NJ: Free Press, 1997).

3. R. Edward Bashaw and E. Stephen Grant, "Exploring the Distinctive Nature of Work Commitments: Their Relationships with Personal Characteristics, Job Performance, and Propensity to Leave," *Journal of Personal Selling and Sales Management* 14, no. 2 (1994): 41–56; and *"The Value of Work-Life,"WFD website,* http://www.wfd.com/worklife/commitpays.htm.

4. Tim Schooley, "Study Correlates Investment Value with Management of 'Human Capital'," *bizjournals.com website,* April 10, 2000, http://www.bizjournals.com/pittsburgh/stories/2000/04/10/focus4.html.

5. Doug Grisaffe, "Understanding and Managing Linkages of Information Within Your Organization," presented at Walker Information Global Network member training, Indianapolis, IN, June 22, 2000.

6. Ibid.

7. Metapraxis, "A Means to an End?" *Business Consultancy* (April 1998); http://www.metapraxis.com/publications/magazine/A_means_to_an_end/A_means_to_an_end.htm.

8. Quoted in Nina Munk, "How Levi's Trashed a Great Brand," *Fortune* (April 12, 1999); http://library.northernlight.com/SG19990714190000281 (December 15, 2000).

9. Levi Strauss & Company Profile, *Hoovers online,* December 2000, http://hoovers.com/premium/profile.

10. Quoted in Munk, "How Levi's Trashed a Great Brand."

11. Ibid.

12. Ibid.

13. Levi Strauss & Company Profile, *Hoovers Online.*

14. Munk, "How Levi's Trashed a Great Brand."

15. Lisa Fasig, "LensCrafters CEO Has Uncommon Vision," *Cincinnati Enquirer,* March 21, 1999.

16. Time Corp., a division of Radiant Systems, "LensCrafters—VisionCare Specialists," http://company.monster.com/lens (June 2000).

17. LensCrafters company profile, *Monster.com website,* http://company.monster.com/lens (December 14, 2000).

18. "100 Best Companies to Work for," *Fortune* (January 2000); http://fortune.com.

19. "In the Nation's Tightest Labor Market in Three Decades, Companies Support Causes to Attract and Keep Employees" *Roper Starch in the News,* http://roper.com/news/content.

20. Quoted in Carol Kleiman, "Community Links Boost Employee Morale, Loyalty," *Chicago Tribune* (November 28, 2000).

21. Ibid.

22. Joe Calloway, "Becoming the Brand of Choice," http://www.joecalloway.com/artclbrand.htm.

23. Kleiman, "Community Links Boost Employee Morale, Loyalty."

24. Ibid.

Index